Majoring in Psych:

Career Options for Psychology Undergraduates

Sixth Edition

Betsy L. Morgan
University of Wisconsin - La Crosse

Ann J. Korschgen
University of Missouri

Bianca Basten
University of Wisconsin - La Crosse

WAVELAND

PRESS, INC.

Long Grove, Illinois

For information about this book, contact:
 Waveland Press, Inc.
 4180 IL Route 83, Suite 101
 Long Grove, IL 60047-9580
 (847) 634-0081
 info@waveland.com
 www.waveland.com

Printed in the United States of America

7   6   5   4   3   2   1

This book is dedicated to our students.

— BLM, AJK, & BB

Contents

Preface to the Sixth Edition

O ver 115,000 students graduate every year with a bachelor's degree in psychology. Spending time and energy thinking about what you want to do and how to do it early in your college career can have an enormous payoff once you graduate. This book helps you lay out some of the questions and answers involved in career planning with a psychology degree and emphasizes how best to market the skills you've already acquired. We hope that you utilize this quick, accessible guide to the planning process as a starting point for further exploration.

This is the book we wish we had read when we were in college. It is a book for most of you who will NOT go to graduate school and will ask, "What can I do with a psychology degree?" Although most of the book focuses on career paths that do not require graduate school, two chapters provide a basic overview of graduate school considerations. Although located at the end of the book, we do not want to suggest that graduate school is the culmination or ultimate endpoint for psychology majors. Too often, psychology majors believe that graduate school is the only option after an undergraduate degree.

We hope this book reflects many options for the future. We have all known students for whom never going to graduate school, going to graduate school after many years in the workforce, or going directly to graduate school have been good choices. All these choices depend on individual career goals, as well as on financial and personal circumstances—aspects that change over time for most people.

Throughout the Sixth Edition, we replaced the phrase "he or she" with the pronoun "they" as a generic third-person singular pronoun for inclusiveness and to reflect current American Psychological Association style guidance. In most chapters, you will find small sections labeled #TMYK, which stands for The More You Know. These sections contain information we wanted to highlight as particularly noteworthy or potentially surprising to readers. In addition, we placed the two chapters on graduate school at the end of the book, not because we feel graduate school is the endpoint for psych majors, but to provide an uninterrupted flow between the job-search chapters.

This edition's most notable update is a complete incorporation of the role of social networking in job searches and self-presentation. All the resources and links are current as of this writing. However, we realize links may become outdated at some point after publication; therefore, each chapter includes a "Google is your friend" section with helpful suggestions for finding information related to chapter topics.

To facilitate your reading of the text, we created a section at the end called "Sources" instead of using the traditional American Psychological Association (APA) in-text source citation format. The information we provide that is based on empirical sources is as current as possible. Finally, we provide references and links to particularly important resources for almost every chapter, and each recommended resource is up-to-date at the time of this writing. Knowing that information changes rapidly and links occasionally become inactive, we also suggest Google search terms and phrases for deeper dives into a topic. We hope you use them.

Since some of you may wish to read chapters out of order, information in one chapter may show up again in other chapters. Sometimes we need to read or hear something more than once for it to sink in. You may occasionally feel overwhelmed as you're reading, thinking you can't possibly do everything we present. Don't let that discourage you. Do as much as you can. We also realize there is no one-size-fits-all approach. Many of you may have unique circumstances that prevent you from pursuing all of the opportunities we recommend. Again, don't let that discourage you. Do as much as you can. Whatever your situation, thinking about your future always deserves attention. Let's get to it!

As with all editions, the Sixth Edition of *Majoring in Psych?* reflects the ideas and concerns of many psychology undergraduates. We thank them for their honesty and their desire to craft successful careers. In addition, we would like to thank our amazing editor at Waveland Press, Jeni Ogilvie, for her careful work.

We'd like to hear from you. Feel free to email your comments directly to Dr. Betsy L. Morgan (bmorgan@uwlax.edu), Dr. Ann J. Korschgen (KorschgenA@missouri.edu), and Dr. Bianca Basten (bbasten@uwlax.edu).

Should I Major in Psychology?

I f you ask 10 of your friends or family members whether you should major in psychology, you'll likely receive 10 different opinions. Psychology is a fascinating science, and students choose to be psychology majors for a variety of reasons. Different facets of psychology may appeal to your unique interests and talents. Obtaining a degree in psychology provides you with a solid foundation of the skills that are beneficial in many careers and that are sought by employers. We have designed this book to be a practical guide to finding and securing a career path where you will best display your talents and interests and put your skills to good use. Although we can't tell you whether you should be a psychology major, we can tell you what questions you should ask in order to answer that question for yourself.

What does it mean to major in psychology? Many people tend to associate psychology almost exclusively with the treatment of mental disorders or distress. When you think of the field of psychology, we may immediately think of Sigmund Freud and his couch, or fictional TV characters, such as the FBI profilers on *Criminal Minds*. So we're going start our answer to this first question by pointing out what it *does not* mean to major in psychology. Graduating with an undergraduate degree in psychology *does not* mean you will *be* a psychologist nor (as one of the authors was disappointed to learn early on) will you be an FBI profiler. You must earn an advanced degree, such as a master's, specialist, or doctoral degree, to be a psychologist. To be a practicing psychologist you would also need a license or certification. Currently, slightly over half of the doctorate degrees (PhDs or PsyDs) in psychology are in the clinical and/or counseling area, but the rest span a wide variety of fields (e.g., developmental, industrial or organizational, social, educational, experimental, neuroscience, etc.). Most of the graduate programs in these areas are extremely competitive and expensive. We don't want to frighten you off, but we want you to be sure you've amply explored what your options are with an undergraduate degree in psychology before you get your heart set on being a mental health professional. We also don't want you to overlook the master's programs in applied areas that may be a good choice (e.g., school psychology, industrial or organizational psychology, guidance counseling, social work, etc.), most of which are a two- to three-year graduate school commitment. We'll talk more about these possible career paths in Chapters 9 and 10.

Now that we have given you this potentially disappointing reality check, let's go back to what it actually *does* mean to major in psychology. Graduating with an undergraduate degree in psychology means you'll have a solid foundation of skills that are relevant to just about any career path. In your psychology courses you'll acquire problem-solving skills, communication skills (both written and oral), teamwork skills, project management skills, critical thinking skills, research skills, and too many other skills to list here. Of course, you'll also learn about psychological theories and concepts, but research tells us that you'll have forgotten much of the content of your courses as soon as the semester is over, but don't be alarmed by this. Employers are rarely looking for students who remember developmental psychology theories, but they are looking for students who can write and speak well, who can work well in teams, and who can manage projects.

Therefore, graduating with an undergraduate psychology degree prepares you for work in both psychology-related and psychology-unrelated fields. Many students may choose to be psychology majors because they "want to help people." That's a great reason to choose psychology, but keep in mind there are many ways to help people and you don't necessarily need a psychology degree to do so. Similarly, you don't need to get a psychology-related job to use your psychology degree. In fact, psychology majors are slightly less likely than other majors to work in a job that is directly related to their training. We hope to expand your ideas about what kinds of careers are possible with a psychology degree (Chapter 3) and focus on ways to enhance your "marketability" (Chapter 5).

> #TMYK: If you find it frustrating that you won't have any specific career training when you graduate with your psychology bachelor's degree, we suggest that you consider a different major in which you can develop career-specific sets of skills (e.g., accountancy, radiation therapy, nursing, and/or engineering).

What is the benefit of psychology versus any other degree?
We may be just a tad biased, but we think psychology is incredibly interesting. The truth is, however, that a psychology degree has no benefit over other degrees, particularly other degrees in the liberal arts or social sciences. We've already said this and you'll hear it many more times throughout this book—your best career strategy is to develop a strong set of skills and interests and then market those skills to future employers. Consequently, we'll talk a lot about seeking out internships and other professional experiences that allow you to hone your skills and interests, and ultimately allow you to seek out and shape the career you want.

Now you're only a few pages into the first chapter and we're telling you that a psychology degree won't make you a psychologist, that you actually don't need a psychology degree to work in psychology-related fields, and that many students with psychology degrees work in unrelated fields. That might lead you to your next set of questions. So, what is psychology and why should you be a psychology major instead of a sociology or political science major?

What is psychology? We don't mean to imply that psychology is not a unique discipline. Indeed, psychology is both a distinct and a diverse field. Its focus on the individual as the unit of analysis is one of its key features. Additionally, psychology is a social science and therefore should provide you with a good understanding of the benefits of the scientific method of acquiring knowledge. Before we highlight a few of psychology's other distinctive features, we'd like to review the concept of a good liberal education. Many people mistakenly think of politics when they hear the terms liberal arts or liberal education. In fact, the "liberal" behind liberal arts refers to freedom of thought. The American Association of Colleges and Universities indicates that a liberal education is

> a philosophy of education that empowers individuals, liberates the mind from ignorance, and cultivates social responsibility. Characterized by challenging encounters with important issues, and more a way of studying than specific content, liberal education can occur at all types of colleges and universities. [...] Quality liberal education prepares students for active participation in the private and public sectors, in a diverse democracy, and in an even more diverse global community. It has the strongest impact when studies reach beyond the classroom to the larger community, asking students to apply their developing analytical skills and ethical judgment to concrete problems in the world around them, and to connect theory with the insights gained from practice. (p. 25)

We'd like to think that a well-intentioned student pursuing their education at a well-intentioned institution of higher learning will be liberally educated; in a practical way, a liberal education will help you develop skills that will serve you well throughout your life. We'll return to skills such as these when we discuss employability in Chapter 5.

Although majoring in many other liberal arts fields would likely help you develop these skills just as well, many scholars argue that psychology is special in the *sheer number* of skills and range of knowledge it offers. Psychology offers students a wide range of practical and professional skills in addition to a solid liberal education, including skills in literacy, numeracy, and computer literacy; information-finding, research, and measurement; contextual awareness and interpersonal awareness; and problem-solving, critical evaluation, higher order analysis, and practical applications.

In short, it is the focus on research methodology and psychology as a social science that will enhance your repertoire of potential skills. Indeed, psychologists at all levels of training tend to be interested in understanding, explaining, and predicting how humans (and animals) think, feel, and act. Many of us are drawn to psychology out of an emotional and intellectual interest in humans and humanity. Consequently, we like to think of the discipline as a great combination of heart and head. So, no matter what career you pursue, you will be expected to be able to analyze situations and make intelligent choices. Courses in psychology should help you develop good critical thinking skills to aid in informed decision making.

Why should I be a psychology major? There are several reasons to major in psychology. Psychology might be a good major if you:

- want to signal employers that you have an interest in people and have interpersonal communication skills;

- want to work in human services;

- want to continue on in a psychology-related graduate program;

- want to double major with another field (e.g., biology) to combine several interests;

- find the subject fascinating;

- are planning a career in a field that requires people skills (such as sales or working with children); or

- want to develop quantitative skills for use in a variety of social science research settings.

Those are just a few reasons why a psychology major might be a good choice for you, although we want to reiterate that none of these reasons mean you HAVE to *major* in psychology. (Psychology also makes a good minor or emphasis because it nicely complements many other fields.) Psychology is a great option for a major if you want a broad, well-rounded degree. Because psychology is a diverse field, it offers many opportunities. *But*, as we've said before, you must play an active role in defining how it will work toward your own career plans.

Nationally, we know that psychology has been among the top 10 most popular majors for several decades. According to the National Center for Education Statistics, over 115,000 students per year are expected to graduate with degrees in psychology for many years to come. Undergraduate psychology majors in the U.S. tend to be predominately female (~80%) and European American (~55%). National data suggest that most psychology majors end up working in health-related fields, administrative/clerical jobs, and social or professional services.

Is it good that psychology is such a popular undergraduate degree? It is good that people recognize psychology as an important and versatile field. It *may* not be good for you personally as it means there will be many other psychology majors competing with you for jobs and/or graduate school admissions.

More discouraging is the fact that roughly only half of the psychology graduates reported that a four-year degree was required for their current job (this number worsens in hard economic times). The other half reported that they were currently working in a job that only required a two-year degree or no undergraduate degree at all. This sentiment may reflect that undergraduates (in many fields) tend to have unrealistic expectations about the roles they'll play in their first jobs. On the positive side, the majority of psychology graduates reported they were in jobs that held career potential, and even more reported that their current job built on skills from past jobs. These last findings suggest that these college graduates expected their career prospects to improve.

All this means that *if* you choose psychology as a major, you may have to "defend" your choice to many people, perhaps including yourself. It is our opinion that your best defense is to be knowledgeable about the field and its applications, so keep reading!

What if I really want to be a mental health professional?
You will have to get an advanced degree and get licensed in order to practice as a psychologist. In Chapters 9 and 10 we discuss graduate school issues. It's possible that you may be able to be involved in some closely supervised counseling-type situations with a bachelor's degree, but you should be wary of situations that place you in positions of responsibility without the proper training. Additionally, even if you think you're good at "helping," you need to be licensed to do so. Bluntly put, you're not qualified to be a mental health professional just because you're good at helping your friends with their problems.

Will I be able to get a job with an undergraduate psychology degree? Nationally, the vast majority of psychology majors are employed and report being satisfied with the length of the time from graduation to employment (usually three months). In your first job after graduation, you might not be working directly in a psychology-related field, but because your employer is likely interested in the skills you acquired as a psychology major, you'll be able to apply much of what you learned in college. This interest is heightened in times when there is a tight labor market. When employers struggle to find applicants trained in their specific fields, they're more likely to turn to applicants who may not have specific training for the job, but do have all the underlying skills necessary to be successful in any job and can easily be trained on the job-specific tasks. Surveys of grads looking for a job during the COVID-19 pandemic found that having a bachelor's degree was more important than having a specific degree in psychology. About 38% of graduates reported that their job was not related to their degree. However, note that during times of recession, psychology majors' options have shown the same level of dip as those of graduates with other majors.

The lists of the top occupations for the 21st century frequently include job titles such as psychologist, counselor, and social worker. The COVID-19 pandemic has further increased the demand for qualified mental health providers. Although these occupations require advanced degrees, there is no doubt that there will also be bachelor's-degree jobs in the future related to psychology.

Will I make any money? Yes, although psychology majors do tend to make slightly less money than many other college graduates. Despite the undeniably negative impact of the COVID-19 pandemic on the job market in general, the average starting salary for individuals with bachelor's degrees graduating in the class of 2021 rose by 2.5% to about $55K. Psychology majors reported starting salaries in the low $50s, although it should be noted that these numbers for psychology majors (current at the time of this writing) are based on a very small response set and may actually be a bit lower.

There are four primary ways to increase your earning potential as a person with an undergraduate degree in psychology. First, psychology majors tend to earn less because many of the psychology-related jobs are in the public sector (e.g., working in a group home or for a county's social services department) and/or are support-level entry jobs. These types of jobs tend to pay less. So, one way to increase your earning potential is to consider private-sector jobs, particularly jobs in the business world (e.g., sales). Second, individuals with advanced degrees in psychology tend to earn more than those with baccalaureate degrees, so getting a master's or doctorate degree may be financially beneficial (but *not* always— read Chapters 9 and 10). Third, students with superior academic records tend to begin at higher salaries. Thus focus on your studies! Finally, many students end up in lower paying jobs because they are unwilling or unable to be flexible about what kind of job they will take or where the job will be. Being flexible about the type of job you're willing to take, as well as where it is located, will enhance your earning potential.

Many students tell us that they "don't care about the money." Although we think it is admirable to choose a career out of compassion and/or interest, we think you *should* care about the money and do whatever is possible to maximize your earning potential within your field of interest. Here are some facts you should think about now: You'll find that your expenses will increase after a few years out of college, especially when you start to have new additions to your life (e.g., automobile, partner, mortgage, children, health care costs, pets, insurance, etc.). Additionally, as mentioned earlier, psychology-related jobs tend to attract a higher proportion of female students than male students. As we hope you are aware, recent female college graduates earn approximately 82 cents to every dollar earned by male graduates (the gap is smaller for psychology majors). A major reason for this difference is choice of major and field of work. Finally, we'd like to remind you that there is ample evidence that a college degree (regardless of gender) is still associated with higher wages and better advancement than high school diplomas.

We want you to make career choices based on accurate information and we want you to be happy with your career and your lifestyle. Chapter 6 is all about earning potential and how to maximize it.

What if I already know what I want to be "when I grow up"?
Well, there are some students who know what career they want to pursue and they do just that. Many are much less certain and that is fine, too. Indeed, most undergraduates change their majors several times during their college career. The important point here is that many roads lead to Rome (as the old saying goes). Even if you decide late that "Rome" is where you want to go, or take some detours, the worst that can happen is that you'll have to spend more time in school.

If you are someone who knows what you want to do, then you probably know whether an undergraduate degree in psychology will serve that purpose. What you might *not* know is that many other undergraduate degrees may also serve your purpose. Most employers and graduate schools are looking for ability and promise. Specific courses can always be acquired when needed. Chapter 4 is about exploring careers, and Chapter 7 is about conducting a job search. Whether you know what you want to do or not, they should help.

After reading all of this, I *still* want to be a psych major. Now, what do I do? We are so pleased you asked. That's what the rest of this book is all about. We have designed it so you should have a firm sense of your options when you're done reading. Chapter 2, entitled "How Can I Be Sure?" is a great place to start. Additionally, don't forget to read Chapter 8; it focuses on some issues you might not think about much as students, such as what to do *after* you get the job or internship. Happy reading!

ADDITIONAL RESOURCES

Chew, S. L. (2021, August 23). The superpowers of the psychology major. *APA Psychology Teacher Network*. https://www.apa.org/ed/precollege/psychology-teacher-network/introductory-psychology/superpowers-psychology-major

American Psychological Association's (APA) education and career information:
https://www.apa.org/education-career

GOOGLE IS YOUR FRIEND—HELPFUL SEARCH PHRASES FOR FURTHER EXPLORATION

- Psychology major alternatives
- Psychology major happiness
- Psychology major pros and cons
- Psychology major career myths

2

How Can I Be Sure?

I s psychology a good fit for you or is another major more appropriate for your interests and your future? Now is the time to find out, not only to save you future effort and wasted course credits but also to help you focus on what is most rewarding for you. Read on, because there are important questions you should be asking yourself. Additionally, there are some interesting steps you can take to help you clarify your choice and then make the most of it! Finally, we've outlined a time line you can use to make the whole process manageable and fun.

If I am thinking of psychology as a major, what can I do to make certain it is right for me? We'll answer this question by identifying several strategies you can implement to develop greater insight into psychology and whether or not it is an appropriate major for you. The strategies are as follows:

Talk to psychology majors. Find students who are psychology majors on your campus. There should be plenty of psychology students, because as we mentioned in Chapter 1, it is a popular major. Ask them to tell you about some of their psychology classes. What were the topics, what projects were required, what was most interesting, what was least interesting? Ask them about their career plans. As they talk, what is your reaction? How do these classes sound? Also ask the students to identify a couple of approachable psychology faculty with whom you could talk.

Talk to psychology faculty. Drop by during their office hours. Ask them about the major, the courses, the career paths of the students who graduate with a major in the field, the expectations of the faculty, and anything else that concerns you. What are your reactions to what they say?

Take some psychology classes. You should take some courses that give you an understanding of the broad theoretical perspectives within psychology (e.g., developmental or social psychology). Deciding on psychology after only taking the introductory general psychology class probably isn't a good idea, especially if you have only taken AP Psychology in high school so far. The introductory survey is usually such a broad overview of the field that it doesn't provide you enough depth to make an appropriate decision about the discipline. Finally, most psychology programs will require you to complete courses in statistics and research design, so don't put those off for too long. Don't forget that other disciplines such as communications, sociology, and criminal justice may have courses that will help you decide if a psychology-related field is for you. Taking a course or two in these types of psychology-related fields will complement your psychology courses nicely and will offer you additional perspectives on similar topics.

Go to the career services office early in your academic career. Ask to speak with an advisor who frequently works with psychology majors. Find out about the typical concerns and opportunities that psychology majors have regarding jobs, internships, and graduate study. Learn about other majors that might also be related to your interests.

Talk to professionals working in the field. You may want to ask the career services staff members for names of professionals working in a field that interests you and then contact them to talk about their work. If you identify a person who works in a job that you might enjoy, ask them about their path and their academic preparation.

What do I gain from following the suggestions you just listed? First, you gain a knowledge base about psychology that allows you to make a more informed decision. Second, you give yourself an opportunity to react to various sources of information about the field, ensuring that you have a broad perspective with which to make a better decision. Finally, by pursuing several of these options, you immerse yourself in the environment of psychology so that you can react on an objective as well as a subjective level to the field and its possibilities. If you have decided to major in psychology, you'll learn about confirmation bias, that is, we tend to seek out information that confirms our existing beliefs and ideas. So as you're gathering more information, remember to not only seek out information about why you *should* be a psychology major but also ask for information about why you *should not* be a psychology major and should choose an alternative major instead.

What issues or questions should I be considering? Sometimes a career path that seems logical and appropriate is still not right because it may not match your values or your ultimate goals. Thus, it is important to think through some of the following issues or questions as they relate to what is important to you and to the kind of person you are and want to become.

Being a psychology major means that the focus of your studies, and probably your subsequent career, will be on people. This has implications that we will explore. Also being a psychology major creates a set of expectations in the minds of many regarding your skills, career options, earnings, and future. It is important to address these expectations as well:

- **Do I like to work with people?** If your answer is tentative, you must explore why. Obviously not ALL psychology majors will work with people, but usually the expectation is that if you majored in psychology you are interested in people. If you are not interested in people from some perspective, we suggest you think again about why you are majoring in psychology.

- **What about working with people who have problems?** Often psychology majors go into careers where they are working with populations, such as delinquent youth or people with disabilities, who have special problems. Other times psychology majors are working with "typical people" who have typical problems, but still problems. It is important to gauge your reaction to this. If you know you like to work with people, but not people with problems, take heed. You may want to avoid one of the typical career paths of psychology majors, human services work.

- **Is a psychology major needed for my goal?** Even if your goal is to find a career in which you work with people, psychology shouldn't necessarily be your major. Many other majors, such as business, health professions, and communications, involve work with people. To make certain that your goals fit comfortably with your academic major, we suggest you start doing some fact finding about alternative career paths, using the help of campus career advisors. If your goal is to get a master's degree in counseling, for example, you will be well served with a psychology undergraduate degree. That is, an undergraduate degree in psychology is a good foundation for graduate work in psychology. Note that a psychology undergraduate degree is also good preparation for graduate and professional schoolwork in other disciplines as well!

• **What should I make of the fact that psychology graduates, generally speaking, earn less money than do many other majors?** If making money is one of your primary career goals, you might want to reexamine psychology as a major. There are no "get rich quick" guarantees that come with this discipline, although some graduates do very well financially. Now is a good time to sort through what you value and why. Oftentimes it is an issue of relative importance. If making money is more important than providing direct service or care to an individual with a problem, then you need to acknowledge that and act on it either by thinking of business career options for psychology majors or by majoring in another discipline. (See Chapter 6 for more on earning potential.)

• **My parents or other family members insist that I NOT major in psychology. They say it offers me no future. What should I do?** The first thing to remember is that it's your life and you who will be responsible for the choices you make. At the same time, it's important to listen to the concerns of your family and to investigate what they say. Certainly share with them the information you learn about psychology from this book and other sources. Majoring in psychology does offer you a future, but whether it's the kind of future you want is for you to decide.

• **Even though I have the interest in psychology, how do I know that this interest will last me my whole career?** It may not. And that's OK. Many people change careers. However, research has shown that if your personality matches your work environment, you'll be more likely to experience a stable and satisfying career. For example, people who have a social personality tend to do best in an environment that involves interpersonal interactions. To decide if a psychology-related career is a good long-term match for you, in addition to taking the steps we outline in this book, you might also want to investigate personality assessment instruments and computerized career advising software, usually offered through career services or counseling and testing offices.

These instruments can sometimes reaffirm your choices or help broaden your knowledge of other appropriate options.

I'm fairly confident that I want to be a psychology major, what's next? Get involved in your field. Ask other psychology majors about clubs or organizations. Usually there is a psychology club on campus that brings in interesting guest speakers. Join it. If there isn't currently a psychology club on campus, think about starting one! There may be other clubs on campus that you might want to investigate and join. For example, if you're interested in human resources or business or communications, there are probably organizations on campus that reflect those interests as well. Find out about any volunteer projects that psychology majors are sponsoring and help out. Talk with psychology faculty about research projects with which they might need help. And, very important, find out about internships and try to have at least one internship experience before you graduate.

Throughout this book, we talk a lot about the importance of getting field or practical experience (such as an internship) as a way to gain skills, make professional contacts, and discover what you like and don't like to do. As suggested, the key is that you need to gain professionally related experiences. In the long run, several dimensions are secondary to the experience. For instance, it really doesn't matter much whether your experience is paid or unpaid (although we realize, it may well matter to you) and whether it's completed for college credit. What matters about professionally related experience (which we often refer to as "internships") is that you work enough hours at an organization to develop skills that are transferable and knowledge about work life that will serve you throughout your career choices.

In Chapters 9 and 10, we stress the importance of research experience as necessary for graduate school preparation. We want to take some time here to stress the importance of research experience even if you do *not* go to graduate school! Research experience is excellent training in logical and critical thought. As an employee you might be called upon to evaluate research as it pertains to your job. In addition, you will be a consumer of research throughout your lifetime because you will need to assess the pros and cons of various issues. We continually use our research training in such situations, including choosing among medical care options, deciding on our children's schooling, making career changes, and planning our financial futures. We use it often when we read blogs, news reports, and social media posts, and you will too. It is a useful skill.

We realize that gaining practical experience in internships and research settings is not necessarily equally accessible to everyone. You may attend a small university in a small town with limited options. You may have to work a full-time job to support yourself and/or your family. You may not have the social connections that allow you to score a coveted internship. You may not feel confident about approaching professors to inquire about research opportunities. Or you may not have the time to engage in research on top of your other responsibilities. As we said in the Introduction, don't let this discourage you. Do the best you can. You can acquire valuable practical experiences in paid positions that on the surface seem unrelated to the field of psychology (more on that in Chapter 5). Also keep in mind that most departments require students to complete a research methods course as part of the psychology curriculum. You will be able to gain valuable research experience in that course, so make it count.

What else might help me now as I plan my psychology major? Plan your coursework. If there are courses you want to take to complement your psychology major, such as courses in criminology, human resources, marketing, or writing, it is essential that you think through which courses you want, when you want to take them, and what prerequisites they might require. If you don't plan ahead, you could end up graduating without some of the academic breadth you need to enhance your marketability.

How can I do ALL that you are suggesting? There's an easy answer to that. Develop a time line, which is a detailed plan designed to help you work through your academic and career interests in a systematic and savvy way. It is like a road map to help you navigate your academic career with the best possible outcomes in mind. Outlined below is a suggested time line. However, you may need to adjust it according to your own personal needs and academic schedule, especially if you are a part-time student.

TIME LINE

First and/or Second Year

- *Decide on whether to major in psychology.* Visit with faculty, talk with career services advisors, and seek advice of current psychology majors, alumni, and employers. Sit in on classes, read about career options, learn about possible internships (see Chapter 5 for more information on internships), and talk with friends and family.

- *If you are already majoring in psychology, discuss your specific interests with a career advisor.* How might you use your interest in psychology in a work setting? See Chapter 3 for examples of some of the jobs available to a psychology major. Explore these options and think through the implications of the choices they offer. For example, your interests will dictate the type of courses you'll want to take, the type of internship(s) you'll want to have, and even the campus clubs and organizations you'll want to join.

- *Identify the courses you'll want to take to complete your major as well as other courses or a minor that will complement your interests.* See which prerequisites exist, when the courses are offered, what special approvals you may need to take the classes, and any other actions that are needed on your part now to ensure you can accomplish what you need to do.

> #TMYK: You will find it beneficial to develop strong technology skills; in particular learn to use a word processing program, statistical analysis software, and spreadsheet software. In addition, the ability to master new applications quickly will serve you well. Almost 40% of college graduates (across majors) indicated they wished they had taken more technology courses while in college.

Third Year

- *Begin to build your resume.* You'll need a resume (a summary of the highlights of your education and work experiences) for applying for an internship. In addition, if you begin to build your resume early in your academic career, you'll be better able to remember the significant aspects of your education and your work experiences that will be important for a future employer to know. See Chapter 7 for tips on how to use online resume sites (such as LinkedIn) to market yourself.

- *Examine internship options and discuss them with an internship coordinator.* Determine if any requirements exist, such as grade

(continued)

point average or year in college, which would affect your application plans. Also identify what special documentation is needed for applying, such as special application forms or a resume.

- **Get involved in campus organizations, volunteer projects, or a research project.** Join psychology clubs, become an APA student affiliate, or join any other organizations that will enable you to learn about your profession as well as to make a contribution of your time and talent. Also, this is a good time to work with a faculty member on a research project.

- **Consider graduate school options.** See Chapter 10 for a suggested timetable to use to examine graduate school possibilities.

- **What else?** Use the resources on campus! Go to career days, browse through the materials in the career library, talk to faculty, search the internet, and learn as much as you can about psychology, your options within it, and how to best use your skills.

Fourth Year

- **Begin your job search.** Use online job search engines, consult the career services' database, participate in on-campus interviews, access vacancy listings, and read Chapter 7 ("How Do I Do a Job Search?").

- If you are considering graduate school, see Chapter 10 for the steps to take.

- **Continue with the activities** we outlined for your junior year, such as being involved in campus organizations, building your resume, and assisting in a research project with a faculty member.

- **What if I have declared a psychology major late in my academic career? What good is a time line?** You may need to accelerate some of the steps we've outlined in the time line, but they will still be useful to you no matter when you declare psychology as your major. We especially encourage you to get to know your faculty members and to have an internship experience.

- **What do I do if I decide that psychology is NOT the best major for me?** It's never too late to make a change. One option would be to switch completely to another major but that may cost you in time and money. Another option would be to finish the psychology major but pick up additional courses in an area of interest. Or you might do internships in your area of interest. We suggest you talk with an academic and a career advisor regarding the best strategy for you.

- **What if I'm more and more sure about psychology and less and less sure about the career options that are available?** We know this is a big issue. Will you get a job? How much money will you make? What kinds of jobs are available? Read on, as we will address these important topics in the next chapters.

ADDITIONAL RESOURCES

U.S. Dept. of Labor website for career exploration:
https://www.careeronestop.org/ExploreCareers/explore-careers.aspx

Website for exploring careers:
https://www.candidcareer.com/

Berkeley's Career Center:
https://career.berkeley.edu/Plan/MajorToCareer

GOOGLE IS YOUR FRIEND—HELPFUL SEARCH PHRASES FOR FURTHER EXPLORATION

• Is psychology right for me?
• Is psychology a good major?
• What are the downsides of majoring in psychology?

3

What Careers Are Available for Psychology Majors?

P sychology majors are highly employable. As we've mentioned before, many psychology students work in areas that you might not originally think of as psychology related. Consequently, you will be well served by expanding your ideas about what you might consider as suitable careers for someone with a psychology degree and by learning how to successfully market your abilities and interests to a wide variety of employers. In this chapter we discuss careers that are well suited for psychology majors, provide a chart of major categories of jobs in which psychology students tend to be employed, and take an in-depth look at three jobs in terms of their responsibilities, salaries, and expected growth.

What kinds of jobs are "right" for psychology majors? As we have stated earlier, research suggests that employers tend to look for global qualities as well as specific skills. Employers look for good communication skills (written and verbal), good interpersonal skills, teamwork ability, flexibility, and analytical skills. Additionally, technological skills (such as basic knowledge of computer hardware and software) are a real benefit to any student in any field. Most psychology programs should serve to improve your abilities in each of those areas. So, in many ways, psychology is a good background for many different types of work.

Psychology is also a field particularly well suited to careers that involve "helping people," which is why many students choose it. So, it is no surprise that many psychology majors work directly in fields where they help people one-on-one. For instance, psychology majors work in group homes, hospitals, nursing homes, correctional facilities, juvenile detention facilities, preschools, shelters, and local, state, and national human services (to name just a few).

However, it is also useful to view your psychology degree more widely and see it as a good general liberal arts degree that sets you up for many potential careers. We don't mean to suggest that you can just graduate with a psychology degree and be offered a job. We do mean to suggest that you can develop a set of skills and interests while in college that are attractive to many employers. We know an employer in banking who specifically recruits psychology majors because he believes they tend to have excellent interpersonal skills. He says he can train them in the specifics of the job, but not in how to interact well with people! APA data from 2019 indicate that ~33% of students with psychology bachelor's degrees have employment with a "for profit" company, ~21% report being self-employed, ~17% each work for nonprofits and in educational settings, and ~11% work in government settings.

We've had more than a few students joke with us about ending up with a career in fast food. These jokes reflect students' genuine worry about their career prospects. But we don't find these jokes particularly funny because they reveal that the students haven't taken the time to learn about sound employment opportunities and may end up resorting to less than advantageous jobs. For example, these students may fall prey to the cynical view that they will never get a good job so be less likely to take the actions necessary to secure good employment with advancement opportunities. Or they may resort to jobs they're familiar with from their high school or college experiences, because they aren't knowledgeable about their other options. Or, ironically, they may avoid working in a fast-food restaurant because they're unaware that fast-food restaurants have many attractive advancement opportunities and should not be written off summarily. (This is *not* a joke; managers' salaries are decent!)

We feel that students who desire to "help people" need to expand what that means to them. Anyone who has worked in sales knows that a good salesperson helps people! Service jobs are some of the fastest growing jobs in the labor market, and service jobs require good people skills. In a similar vein, don't underestimate the importance of your technological skills. A student with a working knowledge of a statistical program such as SPSS will find that this technological skill alone is a genuine foot-in-the-door for some well-paying jobs in finance, marketing, and research.

One of the other issues you may not have thought much about is the difference between "jobs" and "careers." The term "job" tends to reflect any set of responsibilities done to make money, whereas "career" implies the concept of advancement and progression. Research suggests that most people are more satisfied with the attributes associated with careers. Consequently, as you think about your future, we want you to think about building a career rather than just linking jobs. We are not speaking purely to the idea of promotion and advancement. To us, the concept of building a career entails creating a fit between your talents and interests and the responsibilities of your work so you can create opportunities for change and growth.

Finally, graduate degrees open another whole set of additional career choices. The chapters on graduate school will help you think about these options, but we direct you to the career publications and the webpage of the American Psychological Association.

We're trying to get you to think more broadly about the types of jobs for which psychology might be "right." Additionally, we're trying to get you to clarify for yourself what kinds of employment would be OK. What are the qualities of the job that are important to you? What kind of settings do you see yourself in? What kind of pay are you looking for? All of these questions directly affect which types of jobs you'll find interesting *and* how you can use your psychology degree to get there. The list on the following page displays categories of jobs and some individual careers that may be of interest to you.

As you look at the list, you will likely realize how varied those categories of work are, and you should think about *why* some jobs appeal to you more than others. If some of the jobs are unknown to you, it's worth looking into them to see if they might be good career options. To aid in that direction, we'll now take a look at three specific jobs from the list to get a feel for what kinds of tasks and settings are involved. More important, these descriptions inform you of information you can access as a student looking into careers.

LIST OF JOB CATEGORIES

**Human Services Workers
(Community and Social Services)**
Social worker
Program director
Volunteer coordinator

Human Resources
Employee development
Training coordinator
Recruiter

Residential Care
Child disability care
Adult disability care
Elder care

Management and Business
Banking
Sales
Public relations
Hospitality

Scientific Research
Market researcher
Survey researcher

**Student Affairs &
Student Services**
Admissions
Career services
Residential life
Student activities
Alumni/Fundraising/
Development

**Probation/Parole/
Law Enforcement**
Probation/parole officer
Correction officer
Police officer
Treatment spcialist

Education
Childcare worker
Peace Corps
Teacher's aide

Below we look at job descriptions associated with the fields of human services, probation, and human resources. We chose these fields because they are directly psychology related and will give you a sense of the typical work available for psychology majors. Each in-depth description includes information about the most current median wage at the time of writing for each job, that is, the wage at which half the workers in an occupation earned more than that amount and half earned less. So, if an occupation has a median salary of $50K, it means half of all workers earned less than $50K and half earned more than $50K. Usually there are wide wage ranges associated with each occupation, with workers in entry-level positions earning less and workers who have many years of experience and higher levels of education earning more. For each occupation we also address projected future demand up to the year 2029. Note that average projected job demand in all occupations is 4%, with some occupations likely showing more demand and others less.

(Information has been adapted from several sources, including the U.S. Bureau of Labor Statistics' *Occupational Outlook Handbook*.)

■ Human Services Workers

We've chosen this category because it represents jobs that require a bachelor's degree. Other similar categories are "social workers," which traditionally requires a master's degree, and "social and human service assistants," which traditionally requires only a high school diploma.

Work tasks. Human services workers tend to work in a variety of settings and are directed by professional staff. They may offer some direct services such as leading groups or offering one-on-one aid. They often help clients with bureaucratic "red tape." If they work as case aides, they may transport clients to various appointments. Often they are involved in helping to determine a client's eligibility for various programs or services. In general, human services workers deal with people one-on-one and with forms and documents appropriate to the setting.

Work settings. There are a wide variety of settings in which human services workers are employed. Common sites include: group homes, halfway houses, community mental health centers, hospitals, public welfare agencies, nursing homes, facilities for the developmentally delayed, and private agencies servicing specific populations (e.g., individuals with autism).

Salary potential and projected demand. The median salary in 2020 was $69,600 for all workers in the field. Lower-end, entry-level salaries are in the low $40s and higher-end salaries are in the mid-$110s. A bachelor's degree is a minimum requirement. Advancement usually requires a bachelor's degree or a master's degree in a psychology-related field. The projected demand is much greater than average (around 17%), partly due to the aging population and partly due to people seeking treatment for their addictions, as courts refer drug offenders to treatment programs rather than jail. Therefore, demand for managers who direct treatment programs are high.

Qualities of the job you may *like*. Human services workers enjoy the satisfaction of helping others and meeting many different people. They tend to see their work as important. They also enjoy excellent employment opportunities and working a 40-hour week.

Qualities of the job you may *dislike*. Human services workers find that the work can be emotionally draining and that they are under pressure due to understaffing and lack of resources. It can be stressful to know that clients' needs are not being met. They also dislike that the job can involve shiftwork and evening and weekend work. Another drawback is there may be little room for advancement.

Personal qualities helpful to the job:

✓ A strong desire to help others

✓ Patience, understanding, and caring in dealing with others

✓ Good communication skills

✓ A sense of responsibility

✓ An ability to manage time effectively

■ Probation/Parole Officers and Correctional Treatment Specialists

Work tasks. Probation/parole officers counsel juvenile or adult offenders about activities related to their parole (the conditional release from a correctional facility). They help their clients adjust to life outside prison in the hope of minimizing the possibility of future criminal acts. They spend most of their time supervising offenders via phone calls, office visits, and home visits. They test offenders for drugs and offer substance abuse counseling. They also meet with lawyers, law officials, and the offender's family. They are involved in preparing reports and testifying in court.

Work settings. Probation/parole officers work for the probation and parole departments of local, state, and federal governments. About half their time is spent in offices, courtrooms, and prisons, and the other half is spent traveling in the community to meet clients and other individuals involved in the situation.

Salary potential and projected demand. The median salary in 2020 was $69,700 for all workers in the field. Lower-end, entry-level salaries are in the mid-$30s and higher-end salaries in the high $90s. A bachelor's degree is a minimum requirement. Advancement generally requires a master's degree in social work, criminal justice, or psychology, and licensing or certification in social work. The projected demand is average (4%).

Qualities of the job you may *like*. Probation/parole officers like working with people, helping people solve their problems, the challenge and variety of their work, and knowing about the correctional system. They feel as if they have good advancement opportunities (although some require additional education) and good fringe benefits.

Qualities of the job you may *dislike*. Probation/parole officers may dislike having to work evenings and weekends, the pressure from understaffing and heavy workloads, governmental "red tape," working with difficult clients, and the possibility of becoming emotionally drained.

Personal qualities helpful to the job:

✓ A basic concern for people and their problems

✓ Emotional maturity, objectivity, and sensitivity

✓ An ability to make sound decisions

✓ An ability to be fair and firm

✓ An ability to handle responsibility

✓ An ability to work independently

✓ Knowledge of community agencies/services

■ **Human Resources Manager**

We have chosen to describe the manager position because it is typical of an entry-level job in human resources, although many people start out as human resources specialists (median salary ~$64K) before becoming managers.

Work tasks. Human resources managers seek out, interview, screen, and recruit job applicants to fill existing job openings. They maintain contacts within the community and may travel extensively (often to college campuses). Managers screen and interview candidates, and conduct background and reference checks. They often plan orientation and training programs for new employees. Managers may also be involved in salary plans and personnel and benefit budgets.

Work settings. Human resources managers work indoors in offices in virtually every industry: business, health, education, labor organizations, manufacturing, finance, insurance, and government.

Salary potential and projected demand. The median salary in 2020 was $121,220 for all workers in the field. Lower-end, entry-level salaries are in the low $70s and higher-end salaries are in the $200s. A bachelor's degree is a minimum requirement. Advancement is usually contingent on ability and experience. The projected demand is slightly higher than average (6%).

Qualities of the job you may *like*. Human resources managers like their pleasant working conditions and the good salaries and benefits. They like working with people. They also tend to like the ability to travel and being able to interest others in their organization's line of work.

Qualities of the job you may *dislike*. Human resources managers may dislike the difficulty of finding the right person for the position or informing employees that they have been laid off or fired. The occasional need to work long hours to see a project through to a deadline may be a negative factor. Finally, many human resources managers dislike the number of reports they need to complete.

Personal qualities helpful to the job:

✓ Good communication skills

✓ An ability to work as part of a team

✓ Patience, emotional stability, and flexibility

✓ Good computer skills

✓ An ability to function under pressure

These three in-depth job descriptions were selected to give you a feeling about several psychology-related jobs available to job seekers with a psychology degree. More important, they give you a sense of the type of information you can access to learn about almost any career. We've included additional resources below, and you'll want to read this chapter in conjunction with Chapter 7 on job search strategies.

#TMYK: The *Occupational Outlook Handbook* (see below), published by the U.S. Bureau of Labor Statistics, is a great resource and offers an easy-to-search website with detailed information similar to the example provided above (job settings, salary, future demand, education requirements, etc.) about every imaginable job and career path.

ADDITIONAL RESOURCES

Occupational Outlook Handbook:
https://www.bls.gov/ooh/

O*NET Online Career Exploration:
https://www.onetonline.org/

GOOGLE IS YOUR FRIEND—HELPFUL SEARCH PHRASES FOR FURTHER EXPLORATION

- Psychology careers
- Psychology career exploration
- Psychology job outlook
- Psychology jobs in high demand
- Psychology jobs projected to grow in the next decade

4

How Do I Explore Careers?

T here are many ways to get quick and accurate information about career options and many ways to explore specific careers. This chapter highlights several sources of information including faculty members, career services, the library, student clubs, alumni and friends, relatives, practicing professionals, and social networks and other internet opportunities.

Where do I start? As a college student the two best places to start your career exploration are with your faculty and the career services office at your institution. (Almost every school has an office staffed with a person or people to assist students with exploring career opportunities. Though they may differ in name, we will refer to this type of place as "career services office.") However, there are many other great sources of information including the library, alumni, and, of course, the internet. Let's take a look at their offerings.

Faculty. See those "old" people in the corner bent over their lecture notes? They are your faculty. They know something! They can serve as important resources. Most faculty realize that it's difficult and frustrating to make career decisions, and they are often well informed and compassionate; however, individual faculty vary in how useful they can be to you. It will be up to you to find faculty who are both useful and user-friendly. For your part, you should be clear about *what* it is you need so they can determine their role. For instance, if a student comes to Bianca (one of the authors of this book) and says, "I'm totally clueless about what I want to do,"

Bianca will most likely refer the student to the people on campus who have more experience discerning students' interests and aptitudes. Often the career services office has tests and inventories that are a helpful first step in discerning interests. However, if a student says, "I know I like psychology, but I don't know what kinds of jobs are available," or "I want to go to graduate school, but I'm not sure in what," Bianca can help guide the next set of questions, which may help clarify the process, and can point the student toward helpful resources.

Some faculty members don't want to or cannot answer these questions. Don't get discouraged if you encounter this; find someone who will or can. It's our opinion that the best way to encourage faculty members to be more receptive to your questions is to do some legwork beforehand. If you think through your concerns enough to ask specific questions, you'll be more likely to receive helpful answers.

By the way, thinking through your questions is beneficial in general (in college and in the real world). Think about the difference between "I didn't understand your lecture on Piaget" and "I understood that Piaget believed that children go through stages of cognitive development, but you said the structure of the mind changes, and I don't understand how that is related to stages." In interviews and in professional situations, it is often helpful to provide the context for your questions and concerns and to make your questions as specific as possible.

> **#TMYK:** It's shocking to realize, but faculty don't know everything. Remember that most of your faculty members did not build a career with a bachelor's degree in psychology. They probably went to graduate school soon after obtaining a bachelor's degree. So, although they will be a great resource, you should also use other resources to get a full picture of what is available.

Career Services. Most career services offices offer myriad resources to help you. Here is a list of the kinds of things yours may be likely to offer:

1. *Career exploration.* Tests, inventories, and career counseling can help you determine what kinds of careers might be best for you.

2. *Resume preparation.* You can establish your resume online through many career services offices. In that process, the staff will help you review your resume to ensure it best presents your accomplishments. Once it's posted online, you can readily change it as needed, and oftentimes it's made available to employers.

3. *Arranging internships.* Often career services offices maintain lists of employers and organizations in the area who will take student interns. As we've indicated in several places in this book, we think an internship is one of the most important tasks you can do to enhance your career opportunities.

4. *Arranging a job shadow.* Frequently, career services can arrange for you to accompany a professional throughout a portion of their workday. This process of "shadowing" is an excellent way to get a better feel for a job you think might be right for you.

5. *Making alumni contacts.* Career services offices usually have lists of alumni who are willing to be contacted about career opportunities. Frequently, alumni trust their university and place a high value in its students, so they may be prone to hire another alum from the school. Alumni are also helpful because they may have insights into what you might want to do while you're still in school to enhance your employment possibilities.

6. *Job listings and searches.* Many career services offices provide lists or online databases of jobs that are available (usually by major or area). They can also help you find listings for jobs in specific geographic areas.

7. *Employer contacts.* Career services frequently develop relation-ships with specific employers and know their needs and desires. Oftentimes employers will come to campus to inter-view prospective employees or attend career days. This is an excellent (and low-stress) way to explore potential careers.

8. *Graduate school preparation.* Career services usually can help with graduate school preparation, by pointing out graduate school and professional fairs and offering reference guides and information about schools. Additionally, they can provide guid-ance in preparing for graduate entrance exams (e.g., GREs, LSATs, MCATs, etc.), and they may be willing to read and com-

ment on your personal statement. Remember, it pays to start graduate school preparation early in your college career!

9. *Interview practice.* No one pops out of their birth mother "good" at being interviewed! It is a skill and, like all skills, gets better with practice. Many career services offices will run you through mock interviews to better prepare you for the "real thing."

10. *Social networking profile.* Career services can help you make sure you're effectively using social networking and guide you away from inadvertent networking problems such as compromising postings on Facebook, Instagram, or Twitter.

11. *Individualized career help.* Many career services offices offer one-on-one career advising.

Overall, it has been our experience that students have been too reticent to find out what a career services office has to offer. Don't be shy or afraid! March up and say, "I'm trying to decide on a career, can you help me?" or "I'm graduating soon and want to work in Ethiopia, can you help?" Each of the students we know who took the time to learn what their campus's career services office had to offer benefited from the experience.

The Internet. Needless to say, the internet is a powerful career tool. As this chapter is about career exploration, we will focus on those websites. In Chapter 7 on job searching, we will focus more on the use of social networking sites and specific job search engines.

Websites for National Psychology Organizations

• American Psychological Association (APA): www.apa.org

• Association for Psychological Science (APS): www.psychologicalscience.org

• Psi Chi—The International Honors Society in Psychology: www.psichi.org

A Sample of Some Great Places to Visit for Career Exploration (some may involve fees or subscriptions but you will be warned before you spend any money)

• Occupational Outlook Handbook: https://www.bls.gov/ooh/

• O*NET Online Career Exploration: https://www.onetonline.org/

- National Fund for Workforce Solutions:
  https://nationalfund.org/best-practices/career-exploration-tools-and-opportunities/
- Career Spots (your institution may provide full paid access):
  https://www.careerspots.com/

Where else do I look?

Professional clubs or associations. Frequently, academic departments have major clubs such as the "Psychology Club" or honors clubs such as "Psi Chi" or "Psi Beta" that sponsor career-related events such as alumni panels or guest speakers. In addition, Psi Chi has a good publication called *Eye on Psi Chi* and an extensive website (www.psichi.org). Many professional organizations offer student rates. Especially if you are considering graduate school, you might want to join an organization like the American Psychological Association (APA). Their newsletter, *Monitor on Psychology*, has articles of interest to undergraduates and job listings for people with advanced degrees. It's a good way to get a sense of the field. The Association for Psychological Science (APS) also has a student rate and is a good investment for students interested in research-oriented and/or college teaching careers. We provide the website addresses for both APA and APS later in this chapter.

Your campus library. Libraries house many useful traditional and electronic resources.

1. *Guides.* Most libraries have career exploration guides, financial aid guides, and graduate school guides.

2. *Individual searches.* You can always use the library's resources to research specific employers or graduate schools. In other words, it is an excellent place to do your homework on places of interest to you.

Alumni. Even if the career services office doesn't keep a list of alumni, faculty or the alumni office might know some. Alumni are a rich source of knowledge. It is particularly good to hear from those who graduated recently so you can hear about the "current" job market. As always, it is just one person's opinion, so talk to several alums if possible. A blog post regarding the college-to-work transition reads as follows:

One thing I would have done differently in college is try to network a little more. Networking has helped me gain access to new job offers that I otherwise would not have been privy to. Graduating from a large university has helped increase my networking circle, also. If I could go back and do it all over again, I would try to attend more networking events on campus where alumni come back and either speak to students or a meet and greet is set up. You never know when your path will cross with other alumni so it is best to try and meet as many of them as you can. (http://www.careerealism.com/transition-college-career/)

Your family and friends. Don't nod off when your uncle starts to talk about his buddy's son who works in human resources! Networking is alive and well and a major source of job contacts. Use your personal contacts to initiate professional contacts. It is an excellent way to get a sense of several different types of jobs.

Local professionals. If the career services office doesn't line up job shadowing, then do it yourself. We've had several students contact local professionals and ask to shadow or ask to interview the professional about their job. Ask them what they like and what they don't like about their job, and ask them what educational and career path they took to get to where they are now. Students are always surprised by how helpful this is.

> **#TMYK:** Not all career exploration leads you to what you want to do. Frequently, it works more like a process of elimination and you find out what you don't want to do, which is sometimes even more helpful. We've had conversations with the occasional student who returned to campus after a summer internship or a summer job only to report that they realized [*insert former dream job here*] was absolutely not what they wanted to do anymore.

International opportunities? Both employers and students have shown an increased interest in global opportunities for students. Here are good places to start looking for an internship or work experience abroad. Even if English is the only language in which you are fluent, there are multiple opportunities.

- www.peacecorps.gov
The Peace Corps is selective, and volunteers commit to either 3–12 months or 27 months of training and service overseas. (Note that volunteer operations were suspended during the COVID-19 pandemic, so check the website for updates.)

- www.idealist.org
Idealist focuses on nonprofit information and resources.

- https://careers.global/
This is a worldwide job search engine.

- www.jetprogramme.org
The Japan Exchange and Teaching Programme focuses on programs associated with teaching English in Japan.

Educational experiences abroad are also excellent opportunities. If your university or college does not have an international education office, seek out one that does and find out if the credits in their study-abroad courses will transfer to your institution. There are usually semester, annual, and summer-term options available. We realize that international experiences are expensive and may not be accessible to everyone, but note that financial aid and scholarships are often available to cover some of the expenses. Other good resources are www.studyabroad.com and https://www.gooverseas.com/.

Keep in mind that website addresses change fairly often, so don't be surprised if one of the addresses we provide is no longer correct. Needless to say, please remember that the internet is not authoritatively reviewed. Information gained online may be unreliable. It will benefit you to check out the sponsor of any website and the source of information that you are going to use for academic or personal reasons. Always use the critical thinking skills you acquired as part of your psychology training. If a job offer or opportunity seems too good to be true, it probably is!

#TMYK: You should also be aware that there are online employment resources available, specifically for:
- persons with disabilities
(e.g., https://www.dol.gov/agencies/odep),
- people of color (e.g., www.imdiversity.com), and
- the LGBTQ+ community
(e.g., https://outandequal.org/).

Why do I need to use all of these resources? When most of us applied for our first job, we were dropped off in front of a fast-food restaurant or mall entrance, and we shuffled in with the application all filled out in our best handwriting. But most college graduates aren't looking for a "job"; they want a "career." They're looking for a professional opportunity that provides advancement possibilities, interesting work, and decent pay. Most careers don't just show up in your life by the way of a "help wanted" poster in a window. Therefore, you must put in the effort to educate yourself about the possibilities. We guarantee (sorry, no money back) that you will be glad you did!

GOOGLE IS YOUR FRIEND—HELPFUL SEARCH PHRASES FOR FURTHER EXPLORATION

* Psychology careers
* Psychology career exploration
* Psychology internships
* Psychology study abroad

5

How Do I Enhance My Employability?

A s a psychology major, you *will* get a job, unless you do nothing. But there is much you can do *now* that will enhance your career options. In fact, the actions you take while in college determine the type of job you'll obtain later.

What do I need to be doing now about my future employment? First things first. Employers believe that your past performance predicts your future behavior, and many are making hiring decisions based on that assumption. In fact, to learn about your past behavior, more and more employers are using an interview technique called "behavior-based interviewing" in which they ask you to recall behaviors that you have exhibited in the past. Examples of these behaviors could include how you solved a specific problem working with a group of people; how you provided a service to someone in need; or when you demonstrated leadership in a work situation. Employers are interested in knowing about your "track record," which means you should be building a history to carry with you into the future. But how?

Building a history is not as hard as you think, especially when you understand what you need to do. And as you start taking the necessary steps, you will discover that enhancing your "marketability" (which means your ability to sell yourself as an employable candidate to employers) also enhances your academic journey as a student.

So why should I care about my "marketability"? It can make a *big* difference in whether you end up in a job that is a career stepping-stone or a career roadblock.

Have you ever seen someone in a job they hated? Or someone who stagnated in their job position? We have. They're former students who've come back to us saying were too busy as college students to think about their future lives. They failed to take some steps in college to ensure they optimized their opportunities. We don't want the same to happen to you, and it doesn't have to! You can do things now that will lead you to work that will be meaningful and rewarding for you.

What are some steps to optimize my opportunities? The steps below will take some effort, we admit, but the payoff is well worth it. (Take them in the order that makes most sense for you.) We list them and then explain each step more fully later in this chapter.

Steps to Enhance Your Employability

1. Get to know your faculty.

2. Get to know and use resources that can assist you.

3. Volunteer some of your time and talent to campus or community organizations.

4. Participate in at least one (if not more) internship or professionally related experience.

5. Take coursework that supports your plans.

1. **First of all, what does it mean to "get to know my faculty?"** To get to know your faculty, drop by and ask them questions about the course or provide them with comments about the class discussions. Talk with them about the field of psychology and their own career paths. Share with them your concerns about your career plans. Ask faculty members to guide you through an independent study or an internship. You might want to assist them with special projects or research. Faculty members have a lot of wisdom to share. They may also have insights that assist you with your choices. Finally, you may want to ask them to recommend you for a job or for graduate study. You want them to know you well and be aware of your skills and abilities so they can speak with enthusiasm about you. We realize that approaching faculty can be a bit intimidating, but we assure you that (almost) all of us are very nice people who thoroughly enjoy

working with and mentoring students. Don't be shy. Stop by and introduce yourself.

2. **What kinds of resources are there and how can they help me?** As outlined in Chapter 4 on exploring careers, there are many resources available on campus: faculty, alumni, senior students, the library, and career services. All these resources can help you identify your areas of interest and decide on special courses you can take to help you explore these areas more deeply and to enhance your marketability. They can often provide you with the names of alumni who are willing to talk with you about their careers, information about job opportunities in psychology, leads on job opportunities, and internship options.

3. **Why do I need to take time to do volunteer work?** Making an effort to be involved in campus or community projects sends a message about the kind of person you are. Volunteering enables you to help others, to meet people, to develop your skills, and to enhance your marketability. Employers, as we have said earlier, like to know that you have a successful history. Contributing to the community is a good way to help build that history while working on causes that are important to you.

4. **What is an internship?** An internship is a work experience at a placement site appropriate to your career interests. Internships can help you find out what you like (or dislike!), and you may learn a set of skills or how to apply knowledge. An internship signals a potential employer that you have experience and initiative. You may always volunteer or be employed at a place of interest as suggested above, but at many universities and colleges, an official internship can earn you credit toward your degree.

   Why should I bother with an internship? Internships offer many benefits. For example, they enable you to gain relevant work experience before you graduate, they provide you with employers who are often willing to give you strong recommendations, and they enable you to think through your career options and learn about the ambience of a work environment. Sometimes internships provide you the chance to work in a new city, state, or country; they enable you to gain academic credit for your work, and sometimes they pay a small salary; and finally, they enhance your marketability.

We know of many employers who will not even consider recent graduates for employment unless they've had an internship during their undergraduate studies. Below we list the benefits and downsides of internships.

Benefits of Internships

- Gain work experience that is attractive to employers and graduate schools.
- Explore your chosen field of interest and investigate career options.
- Experience hands-on application of classroom knowledge and material.
- Meet new people and establish professional contacts for potential future employment.
- May get to experience working in a new city, state, or country.
- Develop professional skills.
- Learn about important issues within your field of interest.
- May receive financial rewards, and/or stipends.
- Can receive credit toward your degree.
- May receive offer of permanent employment from the internship site.

Downsides of and Barriers to Internships

- May not be the type of work you envisioned or may be more work than you expected.
- Takes time and energy.
- May not be paid.
- Graduation date might be delayed if you do the internship for credit and carry an additionally heavy credit load.
- May come at a busy time (e.g., finals week).
- May need to have your own transportation to get to an internship site and/or to transport clients.
- May need to purchase appropriate clothing to work at some sites.

What kinds of internship sites are available? There is considerable variety in internship sites. It will, of course, be easier to establish one if you are at a school where there is an active internship coordinator (some are housed within academic units). Most colleges or universities have a list of preestablished sites, and most will aid you in initiating a new site if you have someplace you'd like to work. To give you a sense of the type of responsibilities typically given at internships, here is a list of our more popular internship sites:

- Crisis intervention for a telephone hotline
- Education for at-risk youth
- Working with pregnant teens
- Training to help with eating disorders
- Human resource training in personnel issues
- Childcare training and experience
- Domestic violence work (with children or adults)
- Public defender aides or assistance with probation and parole services

Our (the authors') universities are located in regions of at least 80,000 people. Needless to say, if you attend a school in a smaller town, there are probably fewer internship opportunities, just as there are probably more in a larger city. Think about pursuing an internship elsewhere as well. There are exciting national and international internship possibilities. Look into them by asking assistance from your internship coordinator or checking out any number of excellent guides to internship experiences!

Anything you do to develop a set of professional skills is valuable and helpful. Many students are employed in jobs that allow for professional training, just as many students volunteer at interesting sites. It is important to realize that your goals and your supervisor's goals may be different at a job or a volunteer experience than at an internship. Internships have the express purpose of being focused on your professional development and, most important, are designed to give you structured feedback. You may or may not get that from other work experiences. While you may be able to get similar experience at other placements, an internship will be your best bet to secure a position with real professional benefit.

5. **Why do I need to take special courses? Aren't courses in psychology enough?** Psychology courses will be a great foundation on which to add courses to deepen your knowledge base or

skills, but taking additional courses that interest you, signals your specific skills and interests to employers. For example, if you are interested in working with delinquents, you may want to take courses in sociology related to criminology or in political science related to law.

What kind of coursework should I pursue? Elsewhere we mentioned the banker who likes to recruit psychology majors. He said he can train students in the specific skills needed to work in his bank. However, if you were this employer, would you be more excited by a psychology applicant with no banking or financial experience, or by a psychology applicant with some coursework or professional experience? The stronger applicant would certainly be the one with evidence of interests, skills, and training related to banking. You can enhance your appeal to employers in a variety of fields by using coursework to signal your interests or skills.

Below we mention some career tracks and some potential courses to consider. Obviously your choices and options will vary greatly depending on where you are a student; however, you should keep an eye out for courses that enhance your employability.

Of course, along with specific courses, minors and/or double majors are another way to signal your interests and expertise. None of these courses, though, should be at the expense of real experience. We've had students who are seniors and have wanted to stay in college longer to pick up a few extra courses in a field of interest to them. We do not recommend this strategy. Unless you have been advised by an employer or a graduate school admissions committee to take a course or a set of courses, graduating and getting experience will be a stronger path for you in the long run.

What courses should I take in psychology? In other departments? Most undergraduate psychology degrees provide you with a good all-around background in the discipline of psychology. Therefore, the coursework is appropriate to most jobs and graduate programs. In national surveys, psychology majors indicate that the courses they found most helpful after graduation were abnormal psychology and methodology courses, but your needs will vary based on what field you choose.

As we discuss the various career tracks below, we'll mention specific psychology courses if they are applicable and will highlight courses from other departments that you may not have thought about.

STOP! Before you merrily sign up for courses, make sure to check the course requirements. Many courses may not be open to nonmajors or may have prerequisites that you have not yet completed.

Human services and counseling-related fields. If you're interested in counseling-related fields, you'll want to make sure to take abnormal psychology, behavior modification, personality and/or counseling theory, and a course on addictions. However, you should also consider what other departments have to offer (sociology and social work are two potential places to start, if your school has these departments). Consider courses that might build skills (e.g., our speech department offers an interviewing class) or enhance your knowledge of specific populations (e.g., the elderly, adolescents, preschoolers, rehab clients). Additionally, being bilingual is a real plus if it can help you service a particular population. Finally, if your school offers a course in medical ethics, consider taking it.

Business-related fields. Business-oriented students should take courses (or major/minor) in business. Depending on your interests, you should keep an eye out for courses in marketing, management, sales, and courses applicable to human resources (e.g., courses dealing with insurance, compensation and benefits, and personnel issues).

For a career in sales, if you are interested in a specific product or sets of products (for example, pharmaceuticals), take courses that reflect that content area. Additionally, if you are interested in business, consider some business "basics," such as accounting and economics. Depending on your school, some of these courses might also count toward your general education requirements. If your psychology department offers them, consider courses in industrial/organizational psychology, behavior modification, group dynamics, and any course that might serve to enhance your ability to work with people.

Law- or corrections-related fields. Students interested in law-related careers should consider sociology or criminal justice classes, such as delinquency and/or parole, and political science courses on law and legal processes. Students bound for law school should check the specific requirements of the schools in which they are interested and prepare to take the LSAT, a standardized law school admissions test.

Professional health fields (e.g., medicine, physical therapy, occupational therapy, dentistry, and chiropractic). The big issue in preparing for further technical training is making sure you have the proper prerequisites for the program. Most colleges and universities have a person who acts as an advisor for students with these interests. You may also need to prepare to take an admissions test specific to your field (e.g., the MCAT for medical school). Finally, don't be afraid of your psychology degree "looking bad"—it may be the thing that makes your application stand out (as long as you have the grades and the prerequisites to go with it).

Graduate school. Students interested in graduate school in psychology-related fields should look into specific course recommendations or requirements that programs may have and should be particularly careful to take advanced research design and statistics courses as well as courses specific to their interests (e.g., developmental psychology).

Overall, the purpose of coursework in your area of interest is to enhance your knowledge of the field. You will also make contacts with faculty and students who may further aid your career development. Remember that although course content is important, it pales if not accompanied by skills such as good writing, good verbal communication, problem-solving and technology mastery.

What else should I consider? Some additional and important points that can help you increase your chances of finding satisfying work include:

1. **Build your communication skills.** Employers rank oral communication and interpersonal skills as very important in the people that they hire. Being able to talk with people and to get along

with them not only helps in a work setting but in most everything that you do. Seek feedback from others about how to develop these skills. And remember that gaining these skills is not a "spectator sport." You will need practice.

2. **Participate in extracurricular activities.** Being involved in extracurricular activities such as professional organizations, student government, athletics, or clubs signals to an employer that you are a well-rounded person. These activities might also provide specific skills gained through organizing events or working with people who have special needs. In addition to your participation in these activities, how well you're able to talk about and convey the implications of your experiences is a key component of presenting yourself to a future employer.

3. **Try an international experience.** Most colleges and universities provide opportunities to study abroad. Take advantage of them if you can! Employers like to see international experiences on resumes.

4. **Keep an open mind about your possibilities.** One way to enhance your career opportunities is to be flexible about the kinds of work you may see as acceptable or "psychological." Also, keep an open mind regarding your geographic destination. Remember that larger urban areas will offer more numerous and more varied opportunities than might be found in smaller communities.

5. **Develop a positive attitude.** Survey after survey indicate that employers look for and reward positive attitudes. Employers are especially interested in your enthusiasm toward their organization and the work they offer. They prefer a "what can I do for you?" message to a "what can you do for me?" message. Along those lines, employers hire people who are actively engaged in looking for work rather than those who are waiting for something to "come to them."

6. **Be savvy about your job search.** You greatly enhance your chances of finding a terrific job by conducting a terrific job search. For more information on how to do this see Chapter 7.

7. **Clean up your public profile.** You need not have lived like a monk to secure a job, but employers want to hire sensible, reliable individuals. Does your public profile convey that message? Review the following to make sure it conveys professionalism: check your voice mail greeting, make sure your email address conveys a professional character (*beerpongchamp2020@partyperson.com* does not scream "hire me for a responsible position!"), and submit several variants of your name to popular internet browsers and check the image results too. Tighten the privacy settings on your personal pages on sites such as Facebook, Snapchat, Twitter, and Instagram. Audit and edit your online presence regularly.

A study specific to psychology undergraduates' use of Facebook found that a sizable number of the respondents had content of a questionable nature on their publicly viewable accounts. Not surprisingly, studies also show that recruiters and personnel managers use the publicly available information on applicants' social media profiles to make hiring decisions. We recommend tightening your privacy settings and removing photos and posts that suggest characteristics likely to give employers a dimmer view of your professionalism. Finally, once you secure an interview or a job, don't complain about your (potential) employer or colleagues via social networking sites.

8. **Don't obsess over your GPA.** As long as you maintain a certain standard (aim for a B average, but don't worry about that C or D in Econ 101 in your sophomore year), very few employers will care about the specifics of your GPA. A 4.0 GPA isn't any more likely to get you an interview than a 3.1 GPA is, if employers can see that you have the right attitude and skills for the job.

   After reading this chapter, you should feel confident, as a psychology major, that you will be able to get a job. More important, you should feel ready to start planning the strategies to make yourself more marketable so you can end up in the career you want. Keep in mind that each experience you have becomes a part of your total marketability. Don't wait until your senior year to try to understand how it all fits together but rather reflect on your experiences and skills throughout your college career.

GOOGLE IS YOUR FRIEND—HELPFUL SEARCH PHRASES FOR FURTHER EXPLORATION

- Paid internship opportunities
- How do I make myself attractive to employers?
- How do I increase my marketability?
- How to improve my resume
- Social media privacy settings

6

Will I Make Any Money?

Yes, but the answer is not a uniform yes. You will make money, but whether you make A LOT of money depends on several factors, such as the type of work you do. For example, psychology graduates who work in human services occupations are often underpaid (when compared to other college graduates), and they work long hours. They can be rewarded in many other ways, such as in the satisfaction they gain from helping people, and that is often why they stay with that work, but they don't get rich.

Nevertheless, there are many psychology majors who make a lot of money. In fact, several years ago one of our graduates stopped in to say he was just offered a job for $60,000+ with a promise of a six-figure salary in the near future if all worked out as the employer planned. By any measure, that is not a bad salary for someone who graduated less than eight months before the job offer. But you need to know that this job offer was in sales, not in a traditional psychology-related field.

Our point is that you, as a psychology graduate, will have the potential of earning a lot, but it is not a guarantee. Instead, your income is determined in a significant way by the choices you make and by the actions you take to enhance your marketability (discussed in Chapter 5).

If you want to have a hand in shaping your earnings potential, think about how important a good income is to you. How does it weigh against other factors such as assisting others in a human services work setting, living close to relatives, not having to travel frequently, or not having to meet quotas or deadlines? These factors are not necessarily mutually exclusive with earning a high income, but they sometimes are. Often people who earn a lot of money are in business settings, live in large urban settings, travel frequently, and work with tight deadlines. John Menard Jr., the owner of *Menards*, a major Midwestern home improvement store chain, is often cited as saying he finds his psychology degree as or more useful than his business degree because his psychology degree helps him work with people. If you want to earn as much as possible and still do what you enjoy, read on. We will discuss how you can try to make that happen. It is a reasonable goal.

What do I need to know about my income potential as a psychology major? First, you *can* have an impact on what you earn. When you enhance your marketability, you enhance your chances of earning more. This means participating in internship experiences, obtaining a grade point average of 3.0 or higher, receiving strong recommendations from your faculty and others who can speak to your ability, and taking coursework that supports your career interests. Employers tend to "bid higher" for people who appear to have a potential to contribute to their organizations.

> **#TMYK:** It also helps to know what average starting salaries are (see below) when you are negotiating your starting salary with an employer.

What type of starting salary can I expect? This depends on what you would like to do with your psychology background. The average starting salary for all bachelor's level college graduates, ~$55K mentioned in Chapter 1, includes salaries from lucrative careers such as information technology jobs. We gave you an idea of some psych-related starting salaries in Chapter 3, but because salaries change often, we recommend that you look up current starting salaries and starting salaries in specific fields, by consulting the Bureau of Labor Statistics' *Occupational Outlook Handbook* website at www.bls.gov/ooh, or the *Salary Survey*, a quarterly publication from the National Association of Colleges and Employers (NACE). It should be available in the career services office on your campus, and you can find the most recent reports online as well. Finally, there are several good websites for salary information that include information on other relevant considerations such as geographic region and cost of living.

- www.salary.com
- www.salaryexpert.com
- https://www.glassdoor.com/Salaries/index.htm

What are starting salaries with a master's degree or a doctorate in psychology? Starting salaries for applicants with advanced degrees vary widely according to the field in which the applicant chooses to work and may be $10–$30K higher than starting salaries for applicants holding an undergraduate degree. We'll provide more perspective on this in the graduate school chapters. It is important to note that advanced degrees may indicate more earning power over the lifetime. However, any student considering graduate school must carefully consider loan debt as a substantial variable with which to judge salary data.

What if I'm offered a salary that is less than what I believe I deserve? If you are interested in the position, then by all means negotiate with the employer. Explain not only your interest but also your expectations. You can say that you expect a certain amount of money based on the average starting salaries in the field as well as on your experience and ability. Note, however, that you have to be realistic about your salary expectations. If you are in a poor rural area, your chances of negotiating for a higher salary may not be as good as in a wealthier urban area. In other words, it is important to consider the context as you handle this issue.

It is also important to remember that certain parts of the country have higher costs of living than other parts. That job in the city might pay more, but it will also cost you more to live there. Before you accept an offer, ask about the costs of housing, food, insurance, transportation, and clothing. You want to be certain you are making a livable wage.

If I start at a very low salary, will that affect my earnings potential the rest of my life? Not necessarily, unless you remain in the same job and never get merit pay or promotions. But while you are in a low-paying job, it is important to continue to grow and learn so that you'll have improved skills to offer the next employer.

However, it is always best to get the highest starting salary available for the job offered to you.

> **#TMYK:** Research suggests that far too few women even attempt to negotiate salary. In fact, women are less likely to ask for raises, promotions, and better job opportunities, too. Over the lifetime of a career this reticence may lead to missed income and missed opportunity. To risk being simplistic, the key to asking is asking. That is, individuals who try to negotiate usually walk away with some increased opportunities or income. For both the men and women reading this book, it is well worth your time to think about your own feelings regarding negotiating and to learn some practical strategies. We realize it is particularly hard to negotiate for salaries in jobs in the area of human services. The agency is likely to be financially strapped; however, this doesn't mean you should be paid less than a person with the same job just because they "asked" and you did not. Also, as indicated below, salary is not the only form of compensation for which an employee can negotiate. Think about benefits, such as a 401(k) contributions or health insurance premium payments, and on-the-job reimbursements, such as for gas mileage or cell phone calls.

What else do I need to be thinking about? A salary should be only part of the compensation that you receive for your work. You should also be concerned about the fringe benefits such as the health insurance, life insurance, and retirement benefits that an employer offers. Many of us underestimate how much benefits are worth. In general, fringe benefits are worth at least 25–30% of your income. If you do not get these through your work, then you will have to pay for these out of your pocket. If you have a family or a partner, then it is important to inquire about benefits for them as well. Some organizations offer domestic partner benefits for gay and lesbian couples. If this is relevant to you, we encourage you to investigate whether this is a part of the benefit package. If you have children or hope to have children, you might also want to inquire about your organization's in-house childcare facilities. Finally, most organizations find it easier to reimburse employees for their out-of-pocket expenses related to the job as opposed to factoring those costs into employees' salaries. We've had students negotiate for costs important to their jobs such as a cell phone plan or gas mileage.

What should I do if I like the field but don't like the salary? One obvious answer is to consider graduate study, which usually ensures a higher-level entry point into a professional career and thus a higher salary. (See Chapter 9 for a discussion of the financial issues related to graduate study.) Another answer is to consider a career that uses your psychological interests but in a business setting, such as management.

After reading this chapter, you should be aware of the importance of being informed about current salaries, the need for salary negotiation, and some of the other income-related issues involved in choosing a career. There is considerable variation within and across fields, and it is well worth your time to look into ways to maximize your earnings.

ADDITIONAL RESOURCES

Blog post about salary negotiation considerations:
https://www.glassdoor.com/blog/guide/how-to-negotiate-your-salary/
Salary negotiation for nonprofit jobs:
https://www.salary.com/articles/how-to-negotiate-salary-at-a-nonprofit/

GOOGLE IS YOUR FRIEND—HELPFUL SEARCH PHRASES FOR FURTHER EXPLORATION

• Psychology salaries
• Starting salaries in [enter field of interest]
• How to negotiate a starting salary
• Nonsalary benefits/fringe benefits

7

How Do I
Do a Job Search?

To begin, you should have a clear understanding of the type of job you are looking for, why you want to work for a particular organization, and how you can contribute there. Employers want to hire someone who is interested in working for them. They are not interested in someone who is simply looking for any job available. You may ask, how can I know that I really want to work for a particular organization? It's a good question that we will address next. We will also show you how you can use your knowledge of psychology as you conduct a successful job search.

How do I get started in conducting a successful job search as a psychology major? The first step is for you to decide what kind of work you want to do. (Note that Chapters 3 and 4 discuss the steps to take to decide on job options that make sense for you.) By doing this you'll focus your efforts and you'll find it much easier to target the type of employer with whom you want to work.

Remember to start organizing for your job search early in your college career. Waiting until graduation day not only cuts you out of all the great resources and opportunities available to you while you are a student, but it also reduces your ability to be intentional about this very important process.

How do I target and research possible employers? The vast majority of employers use social media and social networking sites to post jobs and recruit employees. There are a large number of online job search engines available (see the URLs at the end of this chapter). We strongly recommend joining the site most frequently used by employers, LinkedIn. Join early in your college career and keep your profile updated. (See the URL at the end of this chapter for a website containing an article with tips and tricks for how to best promote yourself on LinkedIn.) You should also add a link to your LinkedIn profile to your email signature. Here is a quick summary of some suggestions from the article for using LinkedIn for your job search:

- Research companies or nonprofit organizations you may wish to work for through an organization's LinkedIn pages. You can also see which alumni or which people in your network already work there.

- Join groups on LinkedIn to start networking within your intended field of interest. Joining a group will allow you to stay current in your field and start to become aware of the major players and organizations that may be helpful to your job search. Engage in constructive dialogue and show your sincere interest in the field. Do not just ask for people to help you or get you a job. Allow yourself to be mentored and learn through professional conversations. And remember, when you are in the position to mentor someone—pay it forward!

- Seek help. Consider joining LinkedIn groups that are created specifically for job seekers (e.g., "Portland Job Seekers").

- Use the "Save Jobs" function in LinkedIn to track the opportunities you find.

- Sign up for email alerts for new job postings that match your interests. Learn to use the filter functions within LinkedIn to narrow a job search to careers of interest to you. However, don't narrow too much, as job titles vary substantially and you'll want to stay open to a wide range of opportunities.

- Ask for LinkedIn recommendations from the people who know you best, just like with other forms of recommendations. Think of these as very short letters of recommendations.

- Spread the word. Inform your network you are looking for a job by posting an update from your LinkedIn page.

- Do not hesitate to reach out to alumni through LinkedIn and ask them about job opportunities. Not only are most alumni interested in helping, some work for companies that provide bonuses to alumni who help secure new employees. We recommend that you ask them about their own career path, and you may also ask them to critique your resume. We strongly recommend that you connect with alumni before applying for a job so they know you are interested. They may be able to provide information and feedback that will enhance your application.

You may also want to develop another online profile, such as a professional Twitter account or your own website. No matter what your online presence consists of, decide in advance what you want these sites to say about your goals and interests. Maintain a professional image on these sites. As mentioned earlier, employers are occasionally choosing to NOT hire individuals based on concerning information they have found via online profiles. The reality is that you have to play an active role in creating, maintaining, and promoting your online presence to increase your marketability and, ultimately, your likelihood of getting hired for your dream job.

What else do I need to do to find rewarding employment?
You will need a resume that has a positive impact on the employer, accompanied by an attention-grabbing cover letter, and you will need to be an effective interviewee.

How do I design a resume that has a positive impact on anyone?
Organize your resume by listing the most relevant information first. An employer may review hundreds of resumes for a job, so yours needs to stand out by being easy to read and by focusing on the skills, attributes, experiences, and academic preparation that is most relevant to the job for which you are applying. Your resume will have a distinct focus, and that, in turn, reflects positively on you.

You'll want to show the employer that you have a record of success. Employers believe your history will predict your future, so they want to know how well you've done in your past experiences. Specifically, employers want to know what skills or knowledge you've gained from past experiences or how you've contributed to the success of an organization. If you had an internship, or other kind of field experience, you can highlight what you learned from that. For example, if you assisted five at-risk youths in developing better study habits, your resume could state "skilled at motivating young people."

Even if you haven't had directly related experience, you can still discuss the skills you gained that could be transferable to another setting. For example, if you have been a bartender, you might indicate you developed an ability to listen well to people with troubles and learned when it was appropriate to intervene and when it was not (if you did indeed learn this); if you were a member of a restaurant wait staff, you might have designed a more efficient way to arrange the condiment trays, an effort that reveals initiative, creativity, and organizational skills; if you worked in a fast-food restaurant, you likely learned to think quickly on your feet in a rushed situation. These are all examples of transferable talents or skills that will interest employers. Remember, however, that in an interview you must be able to discuss and explain whatever you put on your resume, so don't exaggerate.

What categories of information should I use in my resume?
Career objectives, education, past/current employment, references, special skills, and volunteer activities are all examples of categories. You'll want to select the categories that reflect your experiences and skills. For example, if you've received honors and awards, you might want to include a category titled "Honors and Awards." Or if you've given presentations, you might want a category for those (the same is true for publications or international experience, and so on). It is very important that your resume reflects your uniqueness! You may choose to use your LinkedIn profile as your resume, but it is still a good idea to have a well-formatted PDF version of your resume available to link to your profile or send out via email.

What else is important for my resume? It should be error free! Employers are looking for a way to eliminate resumes (because that is an easy way to make a decision), and the quickest way they have found is to toss out those with spelling or grammatical errors or those that are messy, hard to read, or otherwise not presentable. Proofread, proofread, and then have others proofread.

Many employers say they prefer a one-page resume for new college graduates. However, you can have two pages if your work and other experiences are relevant to the work you desire. Margins, fonts, and format are fun to adjust, but the most important thing is a readable, error-free resume that highlights your specific talents. Also, your resume should always be accompanied by a cover letter (often called a letter of application), whether it is a mailed hard copy or an electronic document submitted online.

How do I write an attention-grabbing cover letter? A cover letter is often the first communication that an employer reads from you, so it should make a good impression. It should let the employer know why you are interested in working with that particular organization. This means you must do the following:

- Address your letter to a specific person rather than to "Sir or Madam" or "To whom it may concern." (If you don't know the person's name and title, call the organization and ask.)

- Explain succinctly why you are writing and why you are interested in their organization.

- Discuss how you're able to contribute to the organization and indicate what you're eager to learn about the organization.

- Don't explain how you learned about the job opening if you're applying for a specific position (this information just wastes valuable space). The only exception would be if you were referred by an employee of the company who is aware their name is being used.

- Write each letter so it targets the specific job and organization for which you're applying; don't send a generic cover letter.

I've submitted my resume and cover letter and haven't heard anything. What should I do? Give the employer some time. Two weeks is appropriate. Then if you don't hear anything, call or email and explain that you have applied, that you are reaffirming your interest in their organization, and ask if they have any questions for you. You might also inquire about their timetable regarding when they will be interviewing and making their hiring decision. Finally, in any communication, be prepared to do more than ask questions. You may want to comment on what appeals to you about the position.

> #TMYK: One reason networking is important is that your contact within the organization may be able to prompt the hiring authority to look at your resume, thereby heightening the visibility of your application.

I have a job interview! How do I prepare? Whether your interview is on campus through the career services office or off campus at the site of the employer, you should prepare for the interview in the same way. Remember that employers are interested in enthusiastic individuals who are eager to contribute to the organization and to grow within it. How do you convey enthusiasm? Remind yourself of the skills and traits you bring to the table and what you can contribute. Armed with this knowledge, you can readily express enthusiasm about yourself. Also, if you have researched the organization, you should be able to communicate specific knowledge of its strengths and why you are interested in being an employee there.

Finally, you can communicate enthusiasm by being prepared for the type of questions you may be asked and by having prepared your own questions. Remember that the company interviews you, but you're also interviewing the company to see if you're a good match. Ask questions that are important to you. "What are the most important values of your company?" "How do you promote diversity and inclusion?" "How do your employees maintain their work/ life balance?" "How do you mentor new employees?" "What are the opportunities for advancement/promotion/additional training?"

What types of questions will I be asked? Employers often use one of two types of interviewing approaches: behavior-based interviewing, which includes questions that are probing and specific, and traditional interviewing, which includes generic questions. We discuss these two approaches below.

What exactly is behavior-based interviewing? Behavior-based interviewing is predicated on the assumption that past behavior predicts future behavior. Thus the employer wants to hear about experiences you've had and how you've handled them. For example, the employer may say to you, "Discuss a time when you had to solve a problem with a group of people. Tell us what happened and the outcome." Now it is important to remember that the employer doesn't want some *general statement* about how your whole life has involved problem solving with groups. Instead, the employer wants you to recount a *specific instance* when you had to solve a problem with a group. This could have been during a class project or in your summer job or in dealing with a family crisis. What is important to the employer is that you recount the context of the situation, discuss your role in it, and explain the outcome. An example of another question is, "Tell me about a time when you assessed someone's need and then provided that person assistance." Basically the employer wants you to answer the questions: "How did you assess their need?" and "What was the outcome of your aid?"

To answer behavior-based interview questions effectively, you will need to think about and be able to talk about situations in your life that are good examples of how you've solved problems, worked with others, handled a difficult situation, or used your creative talents. Employers believe that these situations tell a story about how you will perform your job.

> **#TMYK:** This is true for graduate school interviews too. Additionally, this type of "specific example" is excellent in graduate school application essays.

What is the traditional type of interview? Of course, not all employers are using behavior-based interviewing techniques. Some still use the traditional style, and some use a blend of both. The traditional style interview is usually focused on questions about your perception of yourself (e.g., what are your strengths, what are your weaknesses, why are you the best person for the job) and on hypothetical questions (e.g., "If you were working for us, what would you do if a client yelled at you?"). Employers often believe that because you are a psychology major you will be better able to get along with people, in other words, have strong interpersonal skills. If you think your education has helped you build strong interpersonal skills, then there is nothing wrong with discussing this in your interview. For most employers, an important priority is to hire employees who will get along with others.

How do I prepare for an interview? The best way to prepare is to think about what an employer would most likely want to know about you and prepare the answers you would give. If possible, role-play the questions and your answers with a friend or do it in front of a mirror. If your career services office offers mock interviewing experiences, take advantage of them! Most important, remain calm. There is nothing wrong with taking a minute to gather your thoughts and to think about the answer to a question during the actual interview.

What if an employer asks me a question that seems to be inappropriate? It can happen. If an employer asks you about your marital plans, your religion, your age, your ethnic background, your plans to have children, your weight, or other physical characteristics, then red flags should pop up in your head. Under most circumstances, these questions are not appropriate, and if they are used in making a choice about whether to hire you, then they are illegal. You have three options in terms of how to respond to them:

- You can answer the questions as they are asked, but if you do so, you should be aware that they could be used to discriminate against you.

- You can get up and walk out, saying you're not comfortable with the questions and therefore wish to terminate the interview.

- You can try to analyze the motives of the employer and respond to those. For example, the employer may be asking you about marital plans in order to ensure they are hiring an employee who will stay around for a while. You could respond with something like this:

  "You must be asking me this because you are concerned about how committed I will be to your organization. This is to let you know that I hope to be employed by you for many years."

What else should I expect in an interview? You should be aware that interviews might be conducted in many different ways. Sometimes you might be interviewed by a committee or sometimes by just one person, sometimes on the telephone or a video chat (often long-distance interviews are conducted on the phone or a video chat for initial screening). Be flexible about the format, but still be prepared.

What do I do after the interview? Send a thank-you note to the employer letting them know you appreciated their time and consideration.

What else do I need to know about finding a job? There is a difference in strategy in looking for local employment versus employment in another state or region. LinkedIn and other online job search sites can be used regardless of where you're hoping to find a job, but here are some additional strategies you might consider:

Local. Use your career services office, attend career days and job fairs; volunteer at the organization for which you want to work; look at ads in the local paper; conduct information-gathering interviews to build a network of contacts; identify local organizations using assistance through such agencies as United Way, which usually maintain directories of local human service agencies; use friends and family to put you in touch with possibilities. (See Chapter 4 for other ideas.)

Long distance. Make contact with career services offices in the region in which you wish to locate, contact any friends in that region to see if they have suggestions of people with whom you can talk, and visit there during spring break or during the holidays.

> **#TMYK:** Spring (especially March and April) is the prime time to look for university-related research positions for students who have or will have their bachelor's degree. Spring is the time of year when principal investigators are likely to know about their funding status and are able to post positions.

International. Investigate whether your college has study abroad sites where ongoing relationships are established and where job possibilities might be explored, contact American firms that have subsidiaries in the locations where you wish to go, check with your alumni office to see if any alums from your college are located in the country in which you're interested, and talk with international experts on your campus. Take a standardized language proficiency exam if you speak the language of the country where you're going so your expertise is verifiable.

What happens if I do it all so well that I get several offers and don't know which one to take? If it happens, you can tell the employers you need more time to think through your options, but be aware that many employers are eager to get a response from you as soon as possible. *Under no circumstances should you accept an offer and then continue to interview. That is considered unethical and it will not only damage your reputation but also could damage that of your college as well.* When you are trying to decide on a job offer, we suggest you talk to employees who work at the organizations you are considering in order to get additional insights into their work environment and how well they match with your talents.

Should I apply for a job that only "might" interest me? Our colleagues tell us that they consistently see two problem sets of attitudes from recent college graduates. First, some students preemptively decide they "might" not like a job before applying or interviewing. If this is you and you're offered a job, you can always delay your decision until you've had the chance to thoroughly examine the organization and the specific job. Second, some students don't apply because they don't have all the preferred qualifications. It is not for the job seeker to decide if they are right for the organization; the organization gets to make that decision. So do apply even if you feel like you may not perfectly meet the requirements. The bottom line is: we encourage you to actively apply for all jobs that "might" interest you. Finally, your first job is not your last job. Getting a new job is easier if you're already in a job (even a part-time job). So, think broadly about your potential and be accurately positive about your abilities.

Is there anything else I need to know? We've introduced you to some essential elements of the job search, but there is more to learn and other issues to consider, ranging from appropriate dress for interviewing to prospective employee drug testing. So your preparation does not end with this chapter, rather it is the beginning of one of your most important, if not *the* most important, college projects: to conduct a job search to lead you into a meaningful and rewarding career.

ADDITIONAL RESOURCES

Job search engines:
https://www.linkedin.com/
https://www.indeed.com/
https://www.careerbuilder.com/

Eye on PsiChi article with advice about LinkedIn:
https://www.psichi.org/page/253EyeSpring21Morgan

GOOGLE IS YOUR FRIEND—HELPFUL SEARCH PHRASES FOR FURTHER EXPLORATION

- Resume tips
- Resume mistakes to avoid
- How to write a great cover letter
- Cover letter mistakes to avoid
- Job interview tips
- Common job interview questions
- Questions to ask in a job interview
- How to dress for a job interview
- How to manage multiple job offers

8

I Have My Job (or Internship), Now What?

It's scary to start a new job or internship. It makes you wonder why you ever wanted to graduate college or do anything different. And it's especially scary if you get off to a bad start and don't know how to fix it. This chapter is about avoiding bad starts (or fixing them once they happen) and about taking the trial and error out of on-the-job behavior. Yes, we know that sometimes trial and error is the best way to learn, but it also can hurt. So if you would like to avoid some pain and expedite your learning curve, we offer some ideas about how you can start smart in your career (or in your internship).

What should my first objectives be in my new job? New employees often think their first objective on the new job is to demonstrate their knowledge and skills. Wrong. The first objective is to learn about the culture of the organization and about how best to work within that culture. An organization is like a living being, which functions best when its parts work well together. And it takes more than blind faith to figure out how those parts work. It takes your conscious effort, but the rewards will be worth it.

How do I learn about the culture of the organization? That seems like an overwhelming task! You start by asking questions and LISTENING to the answers. And you start with the easy questions—to find the information you need to know if it wasn't covered in your orientation. Here is a list of some sample questions:

- What is appropriate attire for work here?
- What time are we expected to be here?
- How do people prefer to be addressed?
- What are the ways that special events are celebrated, such as birthdays and awards or recognitions?
- How can I learn about the rules and policies of the organization as they relate to my work?
- What else is important for me to know about the organization and how it functions?

To whom should I be asking these questions? The best people to ask is your supervisor and coworkers and support personnel. Make sure to ask more than one person. When you're new, it's easy to be taken in by one person's agenda or perception. When you hear the same advice from multiple sources, you can begin to trust it.

Speaking of my supervisor, what do I need to know about working with them? You must remember that your supervisor is usually the person who is the final judge regarding whether you are an appropriate "fit" within the culture of the organization. Therefore it's essential that you try to work well with your supervisor. Specifically, you should make the requests and directions of your supervisor your top priority. You should seek feedback regarding your supervisor's expectations of you and try to meet those expectations. You should anticipate the requests made by your supervisor and always avoid surprising them. And under most circumstances you must not talk about your supervisor, especially in a derogatory way. If, for some reason, you have difficulty with your supervisor, you should first go to them and discuss the issue. If that doesn't work and you have made a good faith effort to resolve the problem, you may have to approach another person within the organization. But if you do so, remember that you'll have to live with the possible consequences of "going around" your boss, which could include termination if not a loss of your credibility.

We've seen very talented and popular people within an organization get fired, not because they were not doing their job but because they did not work well with their supervisor. We're not saying the supervisor is always right. But we are saying that the supervisor usually has the final decision about whether you keep your job or not. To think otherwise is not wise. If you can't get along with your boss, you can try to improve your relationship. Or you can talk with the appropriate individuals within the organization about the difficulty you're having but be willing to live with the possible consequences of doing so. Or, at any time, you can look for another job.

> **#TMYK:** A special note regarding internships: One of the benefits of an internship is that you have support. If it is an internship that is college or university related, there should be individuals (faculty, career services, or both) who can help you resolve thorny issues with your supervisor or your work responsibilities. In particular, you should speak up if you feel that you're being asked to do things that are beyond your training or comfort zone (e.g., leading a group by yourself). Please tell someone immediately. In psychology-related fields these kinds of situations have legal and ethical implications.

I get along fine with my supervisor. What else should I be doing? Get to know people within the organization. Ask them to have lunch with you. Find out about their responsibilities, their projects, and their thoughts about the organization. Write down their names and remember them. Treat them in a way that helps create a positive work environment, such as acknowledging their achievements, perhaps by sending them a card. Let them know you are concerned when they have difficulties.

How do I become effective in my specific work assignments? A good question and one that can be answered with six basic steps.

1. **The first step is to get organized and to keep a daily calendar either on your phone/computer or on paper.** It's bad business and can be very embarrassing to miss an important appointment. Stay on top of your schedule. Anticipate meetings or appointments that are forthcoming. Spend time at the end of each day planning for the day ahead.

2. **Know your work priorities.** And then try to achieve your priorities with excellence and energy. Remember that you must excel at your current job before you can even BEGIN to think about the next job.

3. **Evolve with change.** When new ideas come your way, first think about how they might work rather than tearing them apart. In fact, actively seek out new ideas to use for improving your work.

4. **No matter where you work, develop technology skills and continue to update them.** To be effective, you must be able to use the technology used in your company (whether that's "outdated" technology, like email, or new technology, such as specific computer programs used by your organization) and to develop new skills as the technology evolves.

5. **Do all you can to get along well with others.** As we stated earlier, it appears to us that most people are fired from their work because they weren't able to work well with others, not because they lacked the skills to do the job. Seek out the consultation and advice of others, keep people informed, and avoid the easy trap of criticizing the work of others. Instead, focus on how to improve your own work!

   Also, remember that getting along does not mean failing to stand up for what you think is important. If you are asked to compromise your values more often than is comfortable for you, perhaps you might want to think about a new work environment that is more compatible.

6. **Avoid the phrase, "That is not in my position description."** Instead, if you are given an assignment that is more than you can handle, talk with your boss and negotiate the priority that you should give to your new work assignment as it relates to your other responsibilities.

7. **Make sure to tell others when you need help.** Some people end up drowning in their work because they fail to delegate responsibilities to others or because they promise to do more than is humanly possible. If this happens to you, you must talk with your supervisor about getting help and about avoiding this problem in the future.

What else helps me in becoming effective in my career? We highly recommend you consider keeping a *work journal* in which you record the events that happen in your work and your analysis of them. We encourage you to especially attend to your role and your effectiveness. In other words, how did you handle the situation, how could you improve, what were you thinking, what were you feeling, and what psychological theory might explain your behavior and others? We've found that a journal such as this, if maintained over time, can give you a great "window" to your work world and enable you to understand your own perspective.

Another strategy for becoming effective is to *seek feedback* about your work from those with whom you work on a daily basis—especially from those whose work styles and personalities are different from your own. Seek this feedback only if you are prepared to accept it without becoming defensive. When you obtain it, remember that these people have a different approach than you do and thus their approach may not be appropriate for you. However, the fact that they DO have a perspective or approach different from yours might give you new insights into ways for you to become more effective.

What if I hear through the grapevine that someone has a problem with my work? What should I do? We suggest you make an appointment with that person, tell them you've heard they have concerns about your work, and ask for their feedback. It will be a pleasant surprise for them that you want their advice, and it can be a good learning experience for you.

How do I know if I am "on track" with the direction of my career? Start with your personal definition of success. Does success mean moving up through an organization? Or does it mean providing effective, direct service to people in need? Or does it mean providing excellent support to the decision makers? Your definition, not someone else's, should direct your goals. You should also make sure your goals are reasonable given your situation.

Once you've thought through what success means to you, including what you want your career to become and where you want it to happen, think about the steps you'll need to take to build that career. How do those steps break down into monthly and weekly activities? Examples might be:

- What professional journals should you be reading?
- What technical skills should you be developing?
- What advice should you be seeking?

Answers to questions such as these that relate to your goals should guide your work planning and should help you monitor how closely you are "on track" with your career.

How do I keep from making my work my life? Your work will be, or should be, an important part of your life, but just a part. There are also other very significant aspects such as social experiences, time for personal business, spiritual needs, and physical needs. Ironically, the better you attend to those needs, the more effective you can be in your career. To do so, you'll want to create time for your other interests and pursuits, which will involve being willing to set limits and say "no" at work. Many people experience their first position as incredibly time intensive. Some of this commitment is a natural "new job" response. However, you should set limits and strive for balance early in your career. They are important skills to develop, especially for those of us who work in emotionally demanding work.

What do I need to know about saving money? Believe it or not, if you start putting money away now for retirement, even a small amount, you will have the benefit of the money earning compounded interest. This means the interest earned is reinvested— resulting in a cycle of interest continuing to earn interest over time. Your investment will grow, even if you don't add anything to it, and it will reward you in future years. With student loans due and other new expenses cropping up, it's tempting to delay saving for retirement. Please don't. We highly recommend reading up on retirement investments early in your career, even if you're only able to start small and contribute a few dollars each month.

What should I do to allow for job change opportunities? You may find that the job or the career you're in is not a good match for you. That happens to lots of people so don't consider yourself odd. To make a change, however, you may find it helpful to talk with a career counselor, to refocus your resume to reflect the new direction you want to take, to establish a network of contacts in the field you're considering, to take additional coursework, and to join appropriate professional organizations. The advice about networking from the previous chapter still applies after you started your first job!

What surprises new college graduates the most about their new jobs? College graduates are often surprised by the difference between the culture of college and the culture of the workplace. In college, students receive frequent and concrete feedback. In the workplace, employees tend to receive vague and infrequent feedback. In college, students have fairly flexible schedules compared to workers' more set schedules. In college, students have some control over their performance levels, whereas in the workplace the employee is expected to do "A" work all the time. Finally, in college there are few changes in the routine, whereas in the workplace there are constant and unexpected changes. We provide these comparisons to remind you that just as you got used to college, which was strange and different from high school, you will also get used to the workplace, especially if you enter it prepared for a different set of expectations.

Could you list another six million things I should be thinking about? Don't panic. We have listed all these topics to give you a sense of some of the issues with which you'll be dealing. You don't need to respond to them all on the first day, especially when you're just trying to find out where the bathroom is! However, we encourage you to think about the issues we raised and to revisit this chapter in a few months as your career starts to unfold.

When can I start worrying about whether I'm on the right track? Some individuals experience a true "crisis" a few years out of college when they feel as if they haven't made the most of their first 25 years, or haven't hit some classic milestones, or aren't focused about what they want and how to get it. However, for most people, expected and unexpected professional and personal changes are part of every age and developmental stage. As a psychology major, you know that resiliency is the key to navigating life stresses. Each of us can benefit by learning how we tend to deal with stress and by learning adaptive ways to cope with stress.

ADDITIONAL RESOURCES

Hurdles faced by new graduates entering the workforce:
https://hbr.org/2019/04/the-biggest-hurdles-recent-graduates-face-entering-the-workforce

Transitioning from college to working life:
https://social.hays.com/2020/01/29/transition-student-life-to-working-life/

GOOGLE IS YOUR FRIEND—HELPFUL SEARCH PHRASES FOR FURTHER EXPLORATION

- College to job transition
- Adjusting to a new job
- First day on a new job

9

Should I Go to Graduate School?

Going to graduate school takes a lot of time, energy, and money. It also requires aptitude and commitment. Often psychology students think they have to go to graduate school because they mistakenly believe there are no jobs for undergraduate psych majors. If you fall into this category, reread Chapter 3 on jobs with an undergrad psychology degree. You should go to graduate school only if you genuinely know that an advanced degree will be necessary for your intended career. It wastes your time and the graduate school officials' time if you apply on a whim. It is our opinion that you should be crystal clear about why you want *that* specific degree and what you intend to do with it after you obtain it. Chapter 10 deals with the nitty-gritty of applying to graduate school in psychology-related fields. This current chapter involves a series of questions aimed at helping you discern what issues are at hand when considering graduate school.

What are the key issues? The most recent available figures (2018 data) suggest that every year about 28,000 students graduate with master's degrees in psychology and another 6,000 with doctorates. Not all these students started as psychology undergraduates, but when you consider that over 115,000 students graduate every year with psychology degrees, clearly not *everyone* is going to graduate school. It is just not possible or right for most students. Is it right for you? The key issues to consider are: (1) What are my general chances of getting in? (2) Am I suitable for graduate school? (3) Do I want/need to go to graduate school? (4) What kind of graduate school do I want to attend?

1. **What are the odds for admission?** It is important to know the general "state of the union" when it comes to your chances of acceptance. Under no circumstance do we want to frighten you off, but we want you to be aware that graduate school is very competitive and you will need to make yourself an attractive candidate. In the summaries provided in Table 9.1 below, the take-home message is that graduate school in psychology is very competitive and that master's programs are traditionally less competitive than doctoral programs. Note that preliminary data from the last application cycle during the COVID-19 pandemic indicate that some graduate programs might experience an increase in applications. You can use this information wisely to think about your own plans and the attractiveness of your application. For comparison, note that the most recent overall medical school acceptance rate is currently at 42%.

TABLE 9.1   Selected data on acceptance rates by type of degree and specialty (APA, 2019)

Speciality	Type of Degree	
	Master's	Doctoral
Programs potentially requiring licensure:		
Clinical	40%	13%
Counseling	57%	11%
School	56%	31%
Research-focused programs:		
Cognitive	51%	13%
Developmental	51%	14%
Experimental	43%	11%
Industrial/Organizational	39%	14%
Neuroscience	54%	12%
Social	39%	7%

When assessing clinical and counseling psychology graduate programs, there is a tremendous level of variation depending on the type of school and the program's orientation. If you are interested in pursuing graduate work in this area you MUST acquire a much more intensive understanding of the distinctions than this chapter can provide. You should be mindful of licensure and debt load as you consider graduate degree programs. Data from 2016 indicate that master's and PhD students expected to graduate with an average of $75K of debt, whereas PsyD students averaged $160K of debt. Additionally, we know that students of color and other underrepresented groups take on even more student loan debt than other groups. Political discussions surrounding student loan debt forgiveness are in their early stages (at the time of this writing) but are a clear indication that increasing student loan debt is a major concern.

Finally, we have an obligation to comment on the large rise in the number of for-profit education institutions that offer on-campus and fully online graduate degrees. Currently large numbers of psychology master's and doctorate degrees are being awarded at for-profit institutions such as Alliant, Capella, Kaplan, and Walden, to name just a few of the many options. A student must carefully consider both the quality of education and the cost of an education at these schools. The existence of for-profit schools with less emphasis on research is one reason the debt load for practitioners is so high. You must also consider what might happen if a school suddenly closes down in the middle of your program (see reference to an article about Argosy University [Smith, 2019] at the end of the book). This is significantly less likely for public schools or long-running, well-funded private schools than it is for for-profit private schools. If you are thinking about attending one of these institutions on-site or online, you must be a savvy consumer and ask about debt load as well as employability. In addition, if you are thinking about being a practitioner you must ask about placement sites, licensure, and supervision, particularly for programs that are offered completely online. If you are thinking about a career in academia, the prestige and perception of the doctoral-granting institution plays a role. Speak to your faculty and to other professionals before committing your time and money.

2. **Am I an attractive applicant?** Graduate schools are looking for strong students with the initiative and ability to do graduate work. In particular, they need to know that you know why you want that particular degree. Internship and/or research experience is valued because it signals a graduate school that you have a clue about your future endeavors. Strong grades and strong fac-

ulty evaluations also play a major role. You need to show that you can work independently. You must also have the financial ability to pay for the application process and to secure payment (loans, aid, etc.) for the graduate school itself. Finally, you must be a good fit with the particular program in which you are interested.

#TMYK: This may sound harsh, but going to grad school is not just an issue of desire. You must be an attractive applicant. All graduate schools have an admissions process of some sort, and you will have to qualify. We state this here because we often hear students say, "I'll just go to graduate school, if I can't get a job." It is not that easy, and it is not a second choice or a default option. Successful graduate school applicants start their planning early and build a set of experiences and outcomes that display their talents.

Let's take a closer look at several dimensions that you should consider.

Grades. Because many people apply to graduate school, most programs "paper screen" their applicants; that is, they use grades and test scores as quick dividing lines between those who are qualified and those who are not. Therefore, good grades are important. Additionally, good grades show strong study skills that are necessary for graduate school. As a general rule of thumb, any student with a GPA significantly below 3.0 in the major should seriously reconsider graduate school. Once one is above that line there are other issues to consider. First, schools vary in how much importance they place on grades, so you may be applying to a school that will weigh other factors, such as experience, more heavily. Second, the better the school, the stricter the criteria will be. Third, most programs have a minimum GPA required; however, that does not mean if you meet that minimum you will be accepted. Most of the actual GPAs of accepted applicants are considerably higher than the minimum required.

If your grades are not stellar, you'll need to figure that into your graduate school interest and your chances of being accepted. According to the APA, median overall GPAs for master's programs (3.5) are lower than those for doctoral level programs (3.65). Remember that a median number implies that 50% of the accepted applicants are above that number and 50% are below.

Some schools are more flexible about grades. Some weigh other facets more heavily and some will consider improvement in grades. So, if you're like many students and have poor grades for your first year or two as an undergraduate but then show remarkable improvement, your overall GPA will carry less weight. However, the bottom line is that if your grades are not great you MUST offset them with other strong selling points.

Standardized tests such as the GRE. The Graduate Record Examination (GRE) that is required by many schools is often also used as a paper screen. Most schools establish minimum scores for their applicants, but the scores for those actually accepted are higher. In general, good GREs can really help you, but mediocre GREs (as long as they are above the minimum) won't destroy you. You should be aware that some schools make strict GRE cutoffs, whereas others will be more flexible. Also, when you get your GRE scores, remember that the GRE is taken by almost every student interested in graduate school; consequently, the distribution curve is based on some of the strongest test takers in all disciplines. You should study for the GRE and take the practice tests. There are a large number of free and paid resources available online. Expensive preparation courses are not always a better choice than moderately priced self-paced courses. The key is to study early and study consistently.

Note that many schools temporarily waived their GRE requirements during the COVID-19 pandemic, as test-taking sites were closed. Check with graduate programs to see when and if GRE scores are required. Some programs are considering a permanent change to their GRE requirements, but many might return to their prepandemic standards.

#TMYK: If you are interested in graduate training that is not psychology related, you may have to take the test appropriate to that field of study. Some common examples are the LSAT for law school, the MCAT for medical school, and the GMAT for graduate work in business.

Other academic strengths. The other criteria that pull a lot of weight in admissions decisions are less objective than grades and GRE scores. In surveys five major criteria are consistently cited: research experience (for clinical and counseling programs also!), professional experience, strong letters of recommendation, strong application essays, and (if part of the process) a strong showing in the interview. In Chapter 10 we discuss ways to maximize your strengths in these areas.

3. **Motive, interest, and initiative.** After you consider your chances of being admitted to graduate school, you still have the more important question of why you want to go. Again, you must take the time to ask yourself why it might or might not be a good option. "Because I want to be called Dr." is an OK reason, but it probably won't sustain you through several years of graduate work. "Because I want to teach at a university level," "Because I want to be a researcher," "Because I want to be licensed to be a practitioner," "Because I want to be a guidance counselor, a school psychologist, an I/O psychologist" are all good reasons as long as for each statement you can answer the "Why" questions. "Why is an advanced degree needed for this quest?" "Why is this quest important to me?" "Because I can't get a job with a BA" is also a potentially erroneous reason. We realize that job prospects might appear slimmer in the wake of a global pandemic, but if that is your only reason to consider graduate school, please reconsider and revisit the earlier chapters (particularly Chapter 5) on how to make yourself a marketable job applicant, which is helpful advice in any economic climate.

As part of deciding whether you have the initiative and drive for graduate school, you need to consider that most master's programs take two years (some with summers included), and you should plan on at least five to seven years for a doctorate degree. (The median time is actually much longer, but many doctorate-level students start working before they complete their degrees.) Remember, these numbers are the amount of years *after* you've already completed your bachelor's degree. It is a long haul to get a specialized degree. Many students find it invigorating, but many others do not. Only you know if you are interested and passionate enough about obtaining the degree to pursue it. We've watched brilliant students fail to succeed in graduate school. Therefore, we emphasize that you must show a high level of interest and initiative as an undergraduate in order to learn to work independently and show your faculty that you have the necessary drive to succeed in graduate school.

Finally, one of the key reasons you need interest and initiative is that graduate school is *not* like undergraduate school. Most graduate students find graduate-level work to be more demanding in terms of expectations and amount of work. The coursework is more focused, the reading and writing loads are much heavier, and in the later years (especially in a doctoral program) you will be expected to do original, creative, and high-quality work on your own. Graduate school is not just "more years of college."

On the positive side, one of the aspects our students have liked about graduate school is that most of their courses are on topics of interest to them, so they find it easier to stay motivated to sustain the high level of work expected.

4. **Finances.** Graduate school involves financial investment in two ways. First, there is money involved in the application process. Second, and much more substantial, there is the expense of attending graduate school.

   Application costs. Most schools require an application fee that helps finance the large amount of secretarial work involved in the process. Application fees hover around $60 per program. Plus, there are fees involved in taking any of the standardized tests (e.g., the GRE) and fees involved in sending your scores and official transcripts to the various schools. Preparation courses for these tests are particularly costly. Finally, if you visit the schools for interviews or to meet with faculty and see the campus (which we recommend), you will most likely be paying for your transportation and possibly your lodging. At the very least, you should plan on having several hundred dollars invested in the application process alone. (Note there are fee waivers or reductions available for some students, so definitely check if you qualify.)

   Tuition costs and financial assistance. Graduate students pay tuition just like undergraduates do. In fact, at most universities, tuition is higher for graduate students than for undergraduates. Nationally, tuition rates for undergraduates and graduate students have been rising, and experts do not expect the trend to slow down. Fortunately, most graduate students do receive some form of assistance. The most common forms are teaching assistantships, research assistantships, and fellowships. Assistantships require that the student work for the money, and the average workload is around 15 hours a week. Traditionally, master's programs offer less aid to fewer students than do doctoral programs.

The bottom line is that going to graduate school costs money. In addition to the fact that you are paying money out, you are usually not in the workforce so you are losing promotion opportunities. While there is no doubt that the starting salaries and the earning potential of students with advanced degrees are higher than those with bachelor's degrees, it is not a given that graduate school is a good financial investment. Additionally, many students graduate with advanced degrees and then have to start paying off both their undergraduate and their graduate loans. Also keep in mind that the type of graduate training makes a difference. For example, practitioners make more than academics, and, in the counseling field, those with a doctorate degree make more than those with a master's degree. So, we return to our original point: graduate school is most appropriate for a student who wants or needs the specific training offered; however, it is not always a solid financial decision.

5. **What kind of graduate schools are there to consider? Or master's vs. PhD vs. PsyD, what gives?** We are going to give a *very* brief overview of these distinctions. However, you must become very familiar with them. Remember, Google is your friend. In general, master's programs are two-year postbaccalaureate programs (often including summers). In most psychology-related fields, there is very little practical difference between a Master's of Arts (MA) and a Master's of Science (MS). Master's programs will aid you best if they offer very specific training (e.g., school psychology, I/O psychology, rehabilitation counseling, guidance counseling, etc.). As we previously suggested, besides taking less time, they also tend to have slightly lower admission standards. Many master's programs provide excellent training and should not be considered automatically "lesser" than doctorate programs. The big difference lies in

what you want or need the degree to do for you. If you wish to teach at a university level or be an independent practitioner, you will need a more advanced degree.

In general, PhD programs are for students interested in doing research and/or teaching at the university level and/or for students interested in being licensed as clinical or counseling psychologists. PhDs are offered in the many subspecialties of psychology (e.g., cognitive developmental; educational; experimental; industrial/organizational; social & personality; school and more "biological" programs, such as neuropsychology; and the popular clinical and counseling programs). Most doctorate programs take several years to complete, are heavily research oriented, have strict admissions criteria, and are costly.

Doctorates in education (EdDs) are also an option in many fields such as educational psychology or school psychology. EdD programs can differ from PhD programs in terms of coursework and writing requirements and tend to be available in the more applied fields within psychology. Another option is a PsyD program. A PsyD is an advanced degree for practitioners with much less research emphasis than in a PhD program. It is geared to students who want to go into clinical practice. Although PsyD degrees tend to be offered at private institutions and professional schools, there are many public programs as well.

Counseling and clinical programs together account for over half of the psychology doctorates and tend to generate an extraordinary amount of undergraduate interest. There are several routes available for students who are interested in being clinicians (mental health professionals). They can obtain:

- Master's of Social Work (MSW) degree with a focus on counseling or psychiatric social work

> **#TMYK:** MSW programs are not listed in materials put out by the APA because social work programs are not accredited by APA. We recommend the National Association of Social Workers (NASW) as your source for information (www.socialworkers.org/).

- PhD in counseling psychology
- PhD in clinical psychology

- PsyD in counseling or clinical psychology
- MD with subsequent specialization in psychiatry
- There are also a variety of master's level programs in clinical, counseling, and community psychology. They offer counseling training that can lead to licensure. For example, a mental health professional who has an MFCC after their name is someone with a master's or doctorate who has been licensed as a marriage, family, and child counselor, a process that requires 3,000 hours of supervised experience and the passage of a written and oral examination.

It's important to note that there used to be a bigger distinction between counseling and clinical programs. Counseling was seen as training for less clinical populations and clinical was seen as very research oriented. If fact, these fields are extremely similar and both boast some of the most competitive graduate school acceptance rates of any field. An individual interested in this area should examine the specific research and training interest of each school. Whether or not you wish to counsel people, a PhD is a research degree, and you will be expected to have some experience with research and be interested in doing research.

All students interested in counseling-related areas should check on the accreditation of the program and make sure its accreditation has been awarded by a recognized accreditation board. Accreditation is often crucial in securing the supervised training necessary for logging the clinical hours required for licensure. The American Psychological Association accredits doctorate programs but not master's programs. If you're applying to a master's program you will need to check on the credibility of the accreditation board. Furthermore, all practitioner students need to find out what type of licensing preparation they will receive. Licensing is usually a state-level issue, but schools vary in how well they prepare and aid their students to be licensed. As with all graduate schools, be sure to ask each school about the employment rates of their graduates as well as salary data if available. Finally, you should be aware that postdoctoral work (one- to two-year research positions completed after graduate study) is becoming more common and is an expected component of training for many subfields of psychology.

This has been a very brief overview. There is much to know about the different fields and the variation in programs. You will need to call on all of your research skills to become thoroughly knowledgeable about the process. Google is your friend!

What if I'm still not sure about whether I want to go to graduate school? We strongly recommend that you take the time to become sure. There are two primary options for you.

1. **You can complete your college degree, taking care to enroll in courses that will look good to graduate schools, and then go into the workforce.** The key issue here is working in a field that will help answer your question. Many students are "burned out" by attending school and want some time off. However, working as a clerk or server will not help you define your career options. Try to find a baccalaureate-level job in your field of interest (e.g., work as a case worker to get a better sense of what social workers do). You may *never* need to go to graduate school because you'll find work that is right for you. Or, you may choose to go to graduate school much later in your life when you'll have new and different reasons to attend.

2. **You could stay in college longer to get the kind of experience that will help you decide.** Stay in school only if you know of specific experiences or courses that can help you. More school just for "school's sake" will not be particularly impressive to anyone. Stay if you can participate in a faculty member's research. Stay if you can complete your own independent research project. Stay if you can audit or take graduate-level courses that will give you a better sense of the scope and expectations of graduate work.

Will it hurt my chances to take a year or more off (e.g., not go to graduate school right away)? It will certainly not hurt you (and in most cases will even help you) to gain meaningful and relevant work experience before pursuing graduate training. Many students tell us that people have warned them not to take time off. They cite the "you'll never go back" argument. Although "life" can get in the way of graduate school plans, "life" can also shore up graduate school plans. By being clearer about who you are and what you want, you will be a more successful candidate for jobs or graduate school. *But* you must spend the time looking into career options and working in the field, or you will defeat the purpose. So for many students, taking some time off is a good idea, even if they know they want to go to graduate school. Many people go for further education much later in their careers when they can clearly see the need for it, want to make a career change, or have the interest and family situation that allows for it.

We hope this chapter has helped you become more aware of how time-intensive and expensive applying to graduate schools is. If you wait to apply, you may have more to show for yourself after graduating (e.g., completion of a senior project and/or gaining additional experience) and more time to focus on the applications. If you decide to take some time off, it will help you to alert your faculty members that you will be asking them for recommendations in the future. Ask them what their preference is for handling your future request.

Finally, it may surprise you to know that many employers help finance graduate school for their employees. In addition, some employers will allow for some paid time to go toward attending additional schooling.

Now what? If you're sure you're going to apply to graduate schools in the near future, read the next chapter and explore the additional resources and Google searches below.

ADDITIONAL RESOURCES

APA resources for applying to graduate school: https://www.apa.org/education-career/grad/applying

APA used to publish an annual book called *Graduate Study in Psychology*. It is now only offered as an online database. The database allows you to search and compare admissions information for masters and doctoral programs at schools and departments of psychology in the United States and Canada. Check with your college or university to see if they have a paid subscription (see https://gradstudy.apa.org/) or see if your department has an older version of the printed book.

GOOGLE IS YOUR FRIEND—HELPFUL SEARCH PHRASES FOR FURTHER EXPLORATION

- Reasons NOT to go to grad school
- Graduate programs in psychology

- PsyD versus PhD programs
- Master's versus doctorate programs
- Graduate school debt
- APA accredited clinical/counseling psychology programs
- Search for specific graduate programs that interest you and combine your search with key terms, such as "acceptance rate," "tuition cost," "accreditation," and "graduation rates/time."
- GRE practice tests
- GRE fee waivers
- Grad school application fee waivers

How Do I Prepare for Graduate School?

T here are many strategies you can employ to make yourself an attractive graduate school applicant. This chapter first focuses on ways to maximize your chances of getting into graduate school and then covers a time line of tasks associated with applying to graduate school. The chapter concludes with sections on questions to ask of the programs in which you are interested and what to do if you don't get in. Before you read this chapter, you should be sure to read Chapter 9, "Should I Go to Graduate School?" Many of the key issues and admissions criteria are laid out in Chapter 9, whereas this chapter focuses on some of the "nuts and bolts" of the application process. So, from this point forward we are going to assume you are knowledgeable about the basics outlined in the previous chapter.

What steps are involved in applying to graduate school? There are five major steps involved in applying to graduate school:

1. Decide whether graduate school in psychology is right for you (see Chapter 9).

2. Define the area of concentration and degree that you will pursue.

3. Research schools and programs and choose a range of those to which you want to apply (e.g., from stretch schools to match schools to safety schools).

4. Complete the applications to these schools and programs.

5. Attend interviews (if applicable) and make a final decision regarding which school you will attend.

Once you have decided that graduate school appears to be your best bet, you'll need to get busy! It is a complicated and time-consuming process that is made much easier if you have good guidance and are highly organized. In this chapter we'll try to hit the highlights so you'll know what to expect. There are a large number of resources available online that provide valuable and in-depth tips for everything that a graduate school application entails. See the resources and search recommendations at the end of the chapter.

When do I do what? Over the next few pages we've sketched out a basic time line for graduate school preparation. As we have warned, the best time to start is early in your college career. In fact, there is research support for the notion that early planning and its link to graduate school–related activities, such as research experience, benefit applicants. If you are playing "catch-up" to some extent, make sure you are spending your time wisely.

GRADUATE SCHOOL PREPARATION TIME LINE

Your sophomore year:

- Pursue extensive career exploration.
- Take statistics and research design courses.
- Volunteer at an organization of interest to you.

Your junior year:

- Complete an internship or secure professionally related experiences.
- Get involved in local and/or national psychology organizations (Psi Chi). If your school does not have one, get together with some fellow psych students and start a psych club or explore starting a Psi Chi chapter. If there already is a psych club or Psi Chi chapter, get involved and take on leadership roles.
- Consider becoming a student affiliate of APA and/or APS or explore other APA divisions that are related to your career interests.
- If possible, get involved in faculty research and/or think about an independent research project or honors project.
- If you are a student of color, or a first-generation college student, explore if you're eligible for your school's McNair program.

- Start to plan and study for the GREs, making sure to take practice tests. You may want to take the GREs during your junior year or in the summer between your junior and senior years. Career services, your department, or your library probably have information and applications. You can take practice tests on the internet. Visit www.gre.com for more information on how/where/when to take the test. Taking the GRE early is a benefit because there is the option of retaking the GRE to potentially improve your score. GREs are available in a computer format that has the benefit of giving you a wide range of exam sites and dates. Additionally, you can choose to see your score or withdraw your responses without seeing your test score.

- Start investigating graduate programs. Ask your faculty if they know of good programs appropriate to your interests and aptitude. Additionally, your department, your library, and your career services office might have resources to help with this. Several companies (e.g., Peterson's) and/or organizations (e.g., U.S. News & World Report) put out annual guides to graduate programs. These resources often provide information such as rankings of programs, program descriptions, and acceptance rates. As mentioned in Chapter 9, APA publishes a database that is a thorough listing of psychology-related programs. Finally, there is some evidence that "where" you go to receive a practitioner doctorate may be less important than where you go to get a research degree. However, APA accreditation of practitioner doctoral programs is very important.

> **#TMYK:** The APA database of programs is not an easy first step. It provides detailed information about specific programs, but it is too dense for your first swipe through the various offerings. We recommend starting your search elsewhere and then using the APA database to find out more on specific programs that have your attention. If your institution does not have a subscription to the APA database, please know that you can find out similar information by simply digging a bit deeper into each program's own website.

- Visit the websites of schools that interest you. Review the admissions requirements and the curriculum. Explore the research interests of the faculty in the program that interests you. We recommend initiating a literature search on some of the faculty who interest you the

(continued)

most. (Accessing APA's PsycINFO database [https://go.apa.org/psycinfo/] or Google Scholar [https://scholar.google.com/] are the most efficient ways to do this.) Furthermore, we suggest that once you are knowledgeable about their work, you contact them and discuss your interests and career goals. Often, one of these people can serve as an advocate for you in the admissions process if it appears you might be able to work well together.

> **#TMYK:** Like you, faculty are busy people. We recommend against sending form letters, or letters with vague questions, or task requests such as "please send me your most recent publication." Instead, your email should display your knowledge of the faculty member's research and how you may be a good fit. It is reasonable to ask if the faculty member is accepting new graduate students into their lab in the coming year. If you do not get a response, you should assume the individual is busy, not that you have no chance.

Your senior year:

- Visit career services at your school to polish your resume and interviewing skills.
- Take the GREs in early fall (or before).
- Double-check that you have the applications for all the schools in which you are interested. Organize them by application deadline, keeping in mind that financial aid applications are usually due earlier than the program's application deadline. The vast majority of graduate schools have application deadlines between January 15 and March 1, and doctoral programs tend to have earlier deadlines. In addition, graduate assistantships (as a research or teaching assistant) tend to have deadlines that are even earlier than the program deadlines).
- Secure the funds for the application process (see Chapter 9 on costs and potential fee waivers).
- Give your faculty members all your recommendation forms at once (if possible) and give them lots of time to complete them (see discussion below).
- Cast a wide enough net to increase your chances of acceptance. Apply to schools from your "A" list, your "B" list, and even your "C" list. Do not apply to a school if you would not go there if accepted. Geographic variety will usually help your acceptance possibilities.

How do I maximize my chance of getting into graduate school?
Let's review the central criteria for graduate school admission. In general, we talk about quantitative or objective criteria—primarily grades and GRE scores. However, schools also heavily weigh qualitative information that tells them more about you as a candidate. Here are some key areas of nonobjective criteria that most schools consider:

• Letters of recommendation

• Research experience

• Personal statement/Interview (if applicable)

• Professional experience (clinically related public service, work experience, etc.)

• Extracurricular activities

Before we discuss the criteria, we want to remind you that schools vary widely in their admissions standards. Particularly important to remember is that admissions criteria to master's programs are usually less rigorous and less extensive than those of doctoral-level programs. Consequently, depending on your record and your goals, master's programs may be a better fit for you. Additionally, having a master's degree will frequently enhance your credentials if you later decide to pursue doctoral-level work.

What's the big deal with letters of recommendation? People on admissions committees know that each of your faculty members went to graduate school and are, therefore, familiar with its challenges and process. Additionally, your faculty might be involved with graduate admissions at your own school. At the very least, your faculty have watched a lot of undergraduates come and go and have a "reference pool" of students to which they can compare you. In short, your faculty are good judges of your graduate school potential *and* they should be able to tell the admissions committee why you'd make a good candidate.

Bluntly put, your letters have to be strong. Poor or mediocre letters will hurt you. The only way to get good letters is to do good work and to have your faculty members know who you are. You must, must, must get to know your faculty. Start by speaking up in class. You should also visit your faculty during office hours to discuss class material or your career aspirations. Don't just stop by to chat. Most faculty members are busy with a lot of students to attend to, and they will want to see a "point" to the discussion. You should not only ask questions but also share your concerns and aspirations. Tell them about what you do outside the classroom if applicable to your aspirations. If possible, try to take more than one class with the same faculty member so they will have a better chance of knowing you and have more to write about. Offer to be involved with the faculty's own scholarship, or ask them oversee an independent project.

How do I ask a faculty member to write a letter of recommendation? When it comes time to ask for letters of recommendation, do so with care and forethought. If possible, you should arrange a face-to-face meeting with them. If you graduated a while ago and are emailing to ask about a letter, remind the faculty member how they know you. Be specific. You may well remember the faculty member, but, unfortunately, there is a chance they will not remember you without a little prompting. Ask if they know you well enough to write a *strong* letter of recommendation. Sometimes you may need to prod them a bit ("I know you don't know me very well, but I can provide appropriate background information or give you a brief synopsis of how and when our paths have crossed"), but don't push. Again, you don't want a lukewarm letter. If they say "NO," move on to someone else. You want a faculty member to know you well enough to be able to flesh out the persuasive argument. "This student should be accepted to your program, and here are some concrete reasons why." If you are a student at a large university, you or your faculty may wish to involve teaching assistants or other graduate students, who may have gotten to know you better than the senior faculty member has, in the process. Thus it is helpful for you to have these students get to know you.

If the faculty member agrees to write recommendation letters, do everything in your power to make the process painless for them. It is a lot of work to craft a good letter, and most of them will be writing letters for several students. Individual faculty may request different materials to prepare your letter, so be prepared to provide any or all of the following:

• A nonofficial transcript with the courses you have taken from the letter writer highlighted

- Information on any other academic interactions you may have had with the letter writer (e.g., internships, independent study, research, club activities, etc.)
- A current resume/CV
- A copy of your personal statement that you've written for your graduate school application (a rough draft is usually fine)
- All the forms from all the schools at one time. Indicate which ones will be submitted online and which ones will be mailed. (For the latter, you will provide typed, addressed, and *stamped* #10 business-sized envelopes.) Don't forget to fill in your name on the forms and sign the recommendation review waiver statement (Checking "yes" means you will not be allowed to view your letters of recommendation later; checking "no" means you would like to retain the right to view your letters of recommendation.), even on the electronic ones. Check with your letter writers, as some may insist that you check "yes" in order for them to write a letter.
- A table with the name of each school and the deadline date for the letter

Make sure each letter writer knows the names of the schools that will be emailing online letter-of-recommendation links, as sometimes those emails go to the junk mail folder. Provide all of the above well in advance and check with your letter writer as to how much time they will need to complete your letter. Be mindful of semester breaks—nobody wants to write a letter on a holiday. It is appropriate to thank a faculty member for writing letters and an email thank you is fine. Please do not provide a gift, many schools do not allow faculty to accept gifts, and it is part of their jobs to provide letters of reference. However, no matter if you are accepted, the faculty member is most likely interested in the outcome of your application process. Drop them an email and tell them how it went. Tell them your plans and give them occasional updates. That is the "thank you" they most appreciate. We love to hear from our students and tell everyone about their successes.

Why is research experience so important? Doctoral programs are research programs. They'll want to see that you understand the research process and are interested in being a researcher. It's not enough to just find research "fascinating," they'll need to see that you have hands-on experience with the tribulations and joys of research. Master's programs, too, will see research experience as evidence of your interest in and knowledge about the field. All graduate schools will expect you to be critical consumers of research. By the way, it is the research experience that is important; it is less important that the research be directly related to your eventual field of interest. In fact, in a survey that asked current graduate students to identify variables associated with graduate school preparedness, the findings highlighted research participation and quality faculty interactions as two of the most important variables.

There are several ways to get research experience. One of the best ways is to ask faculty if you can work on one of their projects. If you work with a faculty member on their research you should get good training and an insider's view of the process. Another way to get research experience is to do your own. Many schools have honors or capstone experiences where students design and carry out their own projects. If not, many faculty will be willing to advise you on a project of your own design. If you do get involved in research, try to present it. There are undergraduate research conferences as well as undergraduate sessions at the regional and national psychology conferences. Experiencing a professional conference is great training for graduate school; it is also a good way to network. You'll hear about the newest research, meet other undergraduates and graduate students, and potentially meet faculty from the graduate schools in which you are interested. We think you'll find attending conferences less intimidating than it sounds and doing so will make the world of academia less alien and less abstract.

Finally, any student who engages in a research project needs to fully understand its rationale, procedure, results, and implications. It is likely you will be asked about the research during a graduate school interview.

What about relevant experience? You may have wondered why we've harped on internships so often. Experience is a real plus for the job market and for graduate school. You'll be up against older applicants with potentially impressive work experience (especially if you're going into a counseling-related field). The benefit of work experience is that you can use it to help form your career aspirations. Additionally, professional experience may influence the type of training you pursue and/or the research topic you explore once you are in graduate school.

That being said, just having experience is not always enough. The key is to have developed skills and perspective from these experiences. The real challenge is conveying the meaning of these experiences in statements of intent and/or interviews.

> **#TMYK:** This advice also applies to personal experiences. If you have a life experience (e.g., you are a recovering alcoholic, a rape survivor, or the child of divorced parents), AND you choose to share this information with the graduate school admissions committee, the key is going to be showing how this experience has enhanced your ability to be a good mental health professional (or whatever). We would strongly advise not to share personal information that you have not fully worked through on your own first. It is also fine if you choose not to disclose information. Applications are not "bare all" information situations. They are about your presenting what you have to offer, why you want an advanced degree, and why you want it at that specific school.

What about application essays and interviews? Our students find application essays extremely hard to write. They are a sales job about yourself, and most of us aren't used to that type of writing. It is crucial that these essays are well written. Have as many people read them as you possibly can. Have the letter read by any professional who is in a good place to judge (e.g., faculty, career services people, supervisors in related work situations). A friend is better than no one, but they probably won't know what to look for. Do not skip this step! You will be close to the deadline and think, "Oh, it won't matter, this is pretty good." Don't do it! Ask someone to give you feedback.

Essays let the admissions committee learn about you and your experiences as well as your individual strengths (and weaknesses). Your essay should help them get to know you. From a practical standpoint, the biggest mistake we see in essays is errors. Do not let a single typo or grammatical error go by uncorrected! The committee will see errors as indicative of a lack of care and ability. The second biggest mistake we see is boring, linear essays (e.g., "I was born in a small town in . . . [*five pages later*]. Thus, I came to the recognition that being a school psychologist is for me."). While your journey is probably important to you, it is less so to them. Your job is writing a persuasive piece that highlights your strengths and skills and experiences. Try to ground your arguments in a few well-chosen, *specific* examples. Don't make general statements, such as "I am a detail-oriented person" but provide specific examples of when/how you've had to pay attention to detail and how you've honed those skills. Finally, convey your knowledge of their program and how well you'd "fit" with it.

Drew Appleby provided an excellent overview of "kisses of death" in the application process to graduate school. We've included a list below with some of the more common problems. Read the article for an elaboration as to why these are kisses of death and a fuller explanation regarding reference letters.

KISSES OF DEATH IN PERSONAL STATEMENTS

- Avoid references to your mental health.
- Avoid excessively altruistic statements (e.g., "I just want to help people.").
- Avoid inappropriate humor, attempts to appear cute or clever, and references to God or religious issues when these issues are unrelated to the program to which you are applying.
- Avoid spelling or grammatical errors in your application.
- Avoid statements that reflect a generic approach to the application process or an unfamiliarity with the program to which you are applying.

Interviews, too, are the committee's way to get to know about you and see if you are right for their program. In many programs you are being trained to work with people, and your interpersonal skills are of utmost importance. Chapter 7, "How Do I Do a Job Search?" has tips on successful interviews.

Once I've been accepted to one or more programs, what kinds of issues should I consider? Again, this is a brief overview, but you should be an active researcher about the program(s) in question. Below we've listed several questions and statements that might guide your thinking about the various pros and cons of any given program.

- Is there someone with whom you will be "matched" for research interests and who will serve as your mentor?

- What are the employment rates for the program? What percentage of their graduates are working? In what fields? For what level of pay? If applicable, what is their rate of postdoctoral placement?

- What is the average time to completion of the degree at *that* program?

- What kind of financial assistance can they provide? Is it guaranteed? What percentage of their graduate students are assisted? At what level?

- Ask for the contact information for current graduate students and ask them to rate the pros and cons of the program.

- Ask lots of questions to get a feel for the program and whether it will be a supportive place for you.

- For doctoral programs, try to find out about publication rates of their students. What percentage leave the program with publications? How many publications do students typically have?

- If at all possible, visit the schools, arrange to meet with faculty and students, and sit in on a class or two. You will be glad you did.

What if I don't get in? Don't despair if you are not accepted into the program to which you aspire. Consider a different degree (e.g., master's vs. PhD) or a less-prestigious school, and get more experience. See if the schools will tell you why you weren't accepted and work on improving in those areas they cite. If graduate school remains your goal, make sure to continue to enhance your candidacy by pursuing the types of activities we've mentioned throughout this chapter and Chapter 9 (e.g., graduate-level coursework, research experience). Finally, remember that there are decent jobs that don't require advanced degrees. In fact, we recommend that you pursue an active job search while you're waiting to hear from graduate schools so *if* you don't get in, you have some career groundwork laid. Resist the temptation to accept "any" job. Get work in a related field.

After reading this chapter, you should be informed about the crucial steps involved in a well-planned graduate school application process. We expect that you now realize that neither the decision to apply nor the application process is to be taken lightly. If you do choose to apply, we think you'll find that the time and effort you put into the front end will pay off in the long run.

ADDITIONAL RESOURCES

If clinical/counseling programs are your area of interest, we highly recommend Sayette and Norcross's book that is released annually, entitled *Insider's Guide to Graduate Programs in Clinical and Counseling Psychology.*

GOOGLE IS YOUR FRIEND—HELPFUL SEARCH PHRASES FOR FURTHER EXPLORATION

- APA divisions
- Grad school application tips
- GRE practice tests
- How to write a good statement of purpose
- How/Who to ask for grad school reference letters
- Grad school interview tips

Sources

American Association of Colleges and Universities. (2002). *Greater expectations.*

American Psychological Association. (2003). *Psychology: Scientific problem solvers: Careers for the twenty-first century.*

American Psychological Association. (2007). *Getting in: A step-by-step plan for gaining admission to graduate school in psychology* (2nd ed.).

American Psychological Association. (2017). Careers in psychology [Interactive data tool]. https://www.apa.org/workforce/data-tools/careers-psychology

American Psychological Association. (2017). Degrees in psychology [Interactive data tool]. https://www.apa.org/workforce/data-tools/degrees-psychology

American Psychological Association. (2017). Salaries in psychology [Interactive data tool]. https://www.apa.org/workforce/data-tools/2015-salaries.aspx

American Psychological Association. (2019). *Graduate study in psychology summary report: Admissions, applications, and acceptances.* https://www.apa.org/education-career/grad/survey-data/2019-admissions-applications.pdf

Appleby, D. C. (2018). Preparing psychology majors to enter the workforce: Then, now, with whom, and how. *Teaching of Psychology, 45*(1), 14–23. https://doi.org/10.1177/0098628317744944

Appleby, D. C., & Appleby, K. M. (2006). Kisses of death in the graduate school application process. *Teaching of Psychology, 33*(1), 19–24. https://doi.org/10.1207/s15328023top3301_5

Ault, R. L. (1993). To waive or not to waive? Students' misconceptions about the confidentiality choice for letters of recommendation. *Teaching of Psychology, 20*(1), 44–45. https://doi.org/10.1207/s15328023top2001_10

Babcock, L., & Laschever, S. (2003). *Women don't ask: Negotiation and the gender divide.*

Blumenthal, R., & Despres, J. (1996). *Major decisions: A guide to college majors* (3rd ed.).

Bolles, R. (2020). *What color is your parachute? A practical manual for job hunters and career-changers.* [published annually]

Borchard, D. C., Bonner, C., & Musich, S. (2017). *Your career planner* (11th ed.).

Brinthaupt, T. M., Hurst, J. R., & Johnson, Q. R. (2016). Psychology degree beliefs and stereotypes: Differences in the perceptions of majors and non-majors. *Psychology Learning & Teaching, 15*(1), 77–93. https://doi.org/10.1177/1475725716642116

Bureau of Labor Statistics. (2021, September 15). *Occupational outlook handbook.* https://www.bls.gov/ooh/ [continually updated]

Buskist, W., & Burke, C. (2007). *Preparing for graduate study in psychology: 101 questions and answers* (2nd ed.).

Buskist, W., & Mixon, A. (1998). *Allyn and Bacon guide to master's program in psychology.*

Capaldi, E. D. (2000, February). Universe of the master's. *APS Observer, 3.*

Carney, C., & Wells, C. F. (1999). *Discover the career within you* (5th ed.).

Castonguay, C. (2021, April 13). Is COVID leading more people to graduate school? *Keystone PhD Studies.* https://www.phdstudies.com/article/is-covid-leading-more-people-to-graduate-school/

Chapman, J. (2006). *Negotiating your salary: How to make $1,000 a minute* (5th ed.).

Chew, S. L. (2021, August 23). The superpowers of the psychology major. *APA Psychology Teacher Network.* https://www.apa.org/ed/precollege/psychology-teacher-network/introductory-psychology/superpowers-psychology-major

Clark, J. (1991, Fall). Hits and myths about careers in the nonprofit sector. *Journal of Career Planning & Employment,* 43–46.

Collisson, B., Eck, B. E., & Harig, T. (2021). Introducing Gen Z psychology majors: Why they choose to major in psychology (and what they expect to learn). *Scholarship of Teaching and Learning in Psychology.* https://doi.org/10.1037/stl0000249

Conroy, J., Lin, L., & Christidis, P. (2019). How satisfied are psychology-degree holders with their jobs? *Monitor on Psychology, 52*(2), 21.

Conroy, J., Lin, L., & Stamm, K. (2021). A psychology major opens doors. *Monitor on Psychology, 50*(6), 19.

Copeland, D. E., & Houska, J. A. (2020). Did I make the right decision by majoring in psychology? *Eye on Psi Chi, 25*(1). https://doi.org/10.24839/2164-9812.Eye25.1.22

Corey, G., & Corey, M. S. (2018). *I never knew I had a choice: Explorations in personal growth* (11th ed.).

Davis, K. M., Doll, J. F., & Sterner, W. R. (2018). The importance of personal statements in counselor education and psychology doctoral program applications. *Teaching of Psychology, 45*(3), 256–263. https://doi.org/10.1177/0098628318779273

DeGalan, J., & Lambert, S. (2006). *Great jobs for psychology majors* (3rd ed.).

Doran, J. M., Kraha, A., Marks, L. R., Ameen, E. J., & El-Ghoroury, N. H. (2016). Graduate debt in psychology: A quantitative analysis. *Training and Education in Professional Psychology, 10*(1), 3–13. http://dx.doi.org/10.1037/tep0000112

Gardner, J. N., & Van der Veer, G. (Eds.). (1998). *The senior year experience: Facilitating integration, reflection, closure, and transition.*

Geher, G. (2019). Cheat sheet for owning your psychology major. In *Own your psychology major! A guide to student success* (pp. 121–125). American Psychological Association. https://doi.org/10.1037/0000127-012

Geher, G. (2019). How to land (and get the most out of) an internship. In *Own your psychology major! A guide to student success* (pp. 103–110). American Psychological Association. https://doi.org/10.1037/0000127-010

Geher, G. (2019). *Own your psychology major! A guide to student success.* American Psychological Association. https://doi.org/10.1037/0000127-000

Geher, G. (2019). What the pros hope you will learn in your psychology major: Five goals from the APA Guidelines for the Undergraduate Psychology Major. In *Own your psychology major! A guide to student success* (pp. 3–12). American Psychological Association. https://doi.org/10.1037/0000127-001

Harton, H. C., & Lyons, P. C. (2003). Gender, empathy, and the choice of the psychology major. *Teaching of Psychology, 30*(1), 19–24. https://doi.org/10.1207/S15328023TOP3001_03

Helms, J. L., & Rogers, D. T. (2015). *Majoring in psychology: Achieving your educational and career goals* (2nd ed.).

Hettich, P. I. (2010). College-to-workplace transitions: Becoming a freshman again. In T. Miller (Ed.), *Handbook of stressful transitions across the lifespan* (pp. 87–109).

Hettich, P. I., & Helkowski, C. (2005). *Connect college to career: A student's guide to work and life transition.*

Hong, P. Y., Lishner, D. A., Ebert, A., Zimmerman, C., Oechsner, M., & McCann, L. I. (2019). Undergraduates' considerations in declaring either a bachelor of science or a bachelor of arts in psychology. *Teaching of Psychology, 46*(3), 179–186. https://doi.org/10.1177/0098628319848862

Hopkinson, J. (2011). *Salary tutor: Learn the salary negotiation secrets no one ever taught you.*

Hund, A. M., & Bueno, D. (2015). Learning in out-of-class experiences: The importance of professional skills. *Psychology Learning & Teaching, 14*(1), 62–69. https://doi.org/10.1177/1475725714565232

Hunter, A. S., & Meshkati, N. (2020). A descriptive analysis of the perceptions of graduating psychology majors: Reasons for choosing the major, valuable experiences, and suggestions for change. *Scholarship of Teaching and Learning in Psychology.* https://doi.org/10.1037/stl0000232

Huss, M. T., Randall, B. A., Patry, M., Davis, S. F., & Hansen, D. J. (2002). Factors influencing self-rated preparedness for graduate school: A survey of graduate students. *Teaching of Psychology*, *29*(4), 275–281. https://doi.org/10.1207/S15328023TOP2904_03

Keith-Spiegel, P., & Wiederman, M. W. (2000). *The complete guide to graduate school admission: Psychology, counseling, and related fields* (2nd ed.).

Kenkel, M. B., DeLeon, P. H., Albino, J. E. N., & Porter, N. (2003). Challenges to professional psychology education in the 21st century: Response to Peterson. *American Psychologist*, *58*(10), 801–805. https://doi.org/10.1037/0003-066X.58.10.801

Keyes, B. J., & Hogberg, D. K. (1990). Undergraduate psychology alumni: Gender and cohort differences in course usefulness, postbaccalaureate education, and career paths. *Teaching of Psychology*, *17*(2), 101–105. https://doi.org/10.1207/s15328023top1702_6

Kreiner, D. S. (2009). The blessing and the curse of the psychology major. *PsycCRITIQUES*, *54*(29). https://doi.org/10.1037/a0016363

Kressel, N. J. (1990). Job and degree satisfaction among social science graduates. *Teaching of Psychology*, *17*(4), 222–227. https://doi.org/10.1207/s15328023top1704_2

Kuther, T. L. (2020). *The psychology major's handbook* (5th ed.).

Kuther, T. L., & Morgan, R. D. (2012). *Careers in psychology: Opportunities in a changing world* (4th ed.).

Landrum, R. E. (2005). Graduate admissions criteria in psychology: An update. *Psychological Reports*, *97*(2), 481–484. https://doi.org/10.2466/PR0.97.6.481-484

Landrum, R. E. (2009). *Finding jobs with a psychology bachelor's degree: Expert advice for launching your career.*

Landrum, R. E., Davis, S. F., & Landrum, T. (2020). *The psychology major: Career strategies for success* (6th ed.).

Landrum, R. E., & Elison-Bowers, P. (2009). The post-baccalaureate perceptions of psychology alumni. *College Student Journal*, *43*(2), 676–681.

Lawson, T. J. (2018). Tapping into alumni as a source of authentic information and advice on careers in psychology. *Teaching of Psychology*, *45*(1), 67–74. https://doi.org/10.1177/0098628317745452

Lawson, T. J., Reisinger, D. L., & Jordan-Fleming, M. K. (2012). Undergraduate psychology courses preferred by graduate programs. *Teaching of Psychology*, *39*(3), 181–184. https://doi.org/10.1177/0098628312450430

Littleford, L. N., Buxton, K., Bucher, M. A., Simon-Dack, S. L., & Yang, K. L. (2018). Psychology doctoral program admissions: What master's and undergraduate-level students need to know. *Teaching of Psychology*, *45*(1), 75–83. https://doi.org/10.1177/0098628317745453

Lorig, B. T. (1996, March). Undergraduate research in psychology: Skills to take to work. *Council on Undergraduate Research Quarterly*, 45–149.

Madia, S., & Borgese, P. (2010). *The online job search survival guide: Everything you need to know to land your next job now.*

Marrs, H., Barb, M. R., & Ruggiero, J. C. (2007). Self-reported influences on psychology major choice and personality. *Individual Differences Research*, *5*(4), 289–299.

Miller, B. (2020, January 13). Graduate school debt. *Center for American Progress*. https://www.americanprogress.org/issues/education-postsecondary/reports/2020/01/13/479220/graduate-school-debt/

Miller, M. J., & Carducci, B. J. (2015). Student perceptions of the knowledge, skills, and abilities desired by potential employers of psychology majors. *Scholarship of Teaching and Learning in Psychology*, *1*(1), 38–47. https://doi.org/10.1037/stl0000015

Milsom, A., & Coughlin, J. (2017). Examining person–environment fit and academic major satisfaction. *Journal of College Counseling*, *20*(3), 250–262. https://doi.org/10.1002/jocc.12073

Morgan, B., Bald, K., & Basten, B. (2021). LinkedIn: Advice for students and faculty. *Eye on Psi Chi*, *25*(3). https://doi.org/10.24839/2164-9812.Eye25.3.33

Mullane, P. (2021). Should I go to grad school? 5 things to consider in the COVID era. *The Muse*. https://www.themuse.com/advice/grad-school-coronavirus-pandemic

National Association of Colleges and Employers. (2020). *Winter 2020 salary survey*.

Nicklin, J. M., & Roch, S. G. (2009). Letters of recommendation: Controversy and consensus from expert perspectives. *International Journal of Selection and Assessment*, *17*(1), 76–91. https://doi.org/10.1111/j.1468-2389.2009.00453.x

O'Hara, S. (2005). *What can you do with a major in psychology?* O*Net OnLine. https://www.onetonline.org/

Peterson, D. R. (2003). Unintended consequences: Ventures and misadventures in the education of professional psychologists. *American Psychologist*, *58*(10), 791–800. https://doi.org/10.1037/0003-066X.58.10.791

Pinkley, R. L., & Northcraft, G. B. (2000). *Get paid what you're worth: The expert negotiator's guide to salary and compensation*.

Rajecki, D. W. (2008). Job lists for entry-level psychology baccalaureates: Occupational recommendations that mismatch qualifications. *Teaching of Psychology*, *35*(1), 33–37. https://doi.org/10.1080/00986280701818524

Rajecki, D. W., & Anderson, S. L. (2004). Career pathway information in introductory psychology textbooks. *Teaching of Psychology*, *31*(2), 116–118.

Rajecki, D. W., & Borden, V. M. H. (2009). First-year employment outcomes of U.S. psychology graduates revisited: Need for a degree, salary and relatedness to the major. *Psychology Learning & Teaching*, *8*(2), 23–29. https://doi.org/10.2304/plat.2009.8.2.23

Rossi, P. (2011). *Everyday etiquette: How to navigate 101 common and uncommon social situations*.

Sanders, C. E., & Landrum, R. E. (2012). The graduate school application process: What our students report they know. *Teaching of Psychology, 39*(2), 128–132. https://doi.org/10.1177/0098628312437697

Sayette, M. A., & Norcross, J. C. (2020). *Insider's guide to graduate programs in clinical and counseling psychology, 2020/2021 ed.*

Schatz, R. T., & Ansburg, P. I. (2020). Advising psychology majors about graduate school in psychology: Current practices and challenges. *Scholarship of Teaching and Learning in Psychology, 6*(1), 36–45. https://doi.org/10.1037/stl0000165

Shoenfelt, E. L. (2021). An introduction to industrial-organizational psychology master's careers: Successful paths to divergent destinations. In E. L. Shoenfelt (Ed.), *Mastering the job market: Career issues for master's level industrial-organizational psychologists* (pp. 1–15). Oxford Scholarship Online: https://doi.org/10.1093/oso/9780190071172.003.0001

Silvia, P. J., Delaney, P. F., & Marcovitch, S. (2017). *What psychology majors could (and should) be doing: A guide to research experience, professional skills, and your options after college* (2nd ed.). https://doi.org/10.1037/15965-000

Smith, A. A. (2019, March 22). Few options for Argosy graduate students. *Inside Higher Ed.* https://www.insidehighered.com/news/2019/03/22/graduate-and-professional-students-now-closed-argosy-university-campuses-struggle

Stanovich, K. E. (2019). *How to think straight about psychology* (11th ed.).

Sternberg, R. J., Dietz-Uhler, B., & Leach, C. (2016). *The psychologist's companion: A guide to scientific writing for students and researchers* (6th ed.).

Stewart, R., Hill, K., Stewart, J., Bimler, D., & Kirkland, J. (2005). Why I am a psychology major: An empirical analysis of student motivations. *Quality & Quantity: International Journal of Methodology, 39*(6), 687–709. https://doi.org/10.1007/s11135-005-4484-9

Strapp, C. M., Bredimus, K., Wright, T., Cochrane, R., & Fields, E. (2021). Entering the workforce or going to graduate school: Themes in psychology alumni decision making. *Teaching of Psychology, 48*(2), 144–154. https://doi.org/10.1177/0098628320977770

Strapp, C. M., Drapela, D. J., Henderson, C. I., Nasciemento, E., & Roscoe, L. J. (2018). Psychology students' expectations regarding educational requirements and salary for desired careers. *Teaching of Psychology, 45*(1), 6–13. https://doi.org/10.1177/0098628317744943

Tews, M. J., Templer, D. I., Stokes, S., & Forward, V. (2004). Comparing professional schools and traditional clinical program faculty on measures of professional and scientific achievement. *Psychological Reports, 95*(3, Pt 1), 837–840. https://doi.org/10.2466/PR0.95.7.837-840

Thomas, J. H., & McDaniel, C. R. (2004). Effectiveness of a required course in career planning for psychology majors. *Teaching of Psychology, 31*(1), 22–27. https://doi.org/10.1207/s15328023top3101_6

U.S. Department of Education, National Center for Education Statistics. (2020). Digest of education statistics, 2019.

Vespia, K. M., Naufel, K. Z., Rudmann, J., Van Kirk, J. F., Briihl, D., & Young, J. (2020). Yes, you can get a job with that major! Goal 5 strategies for facilitating, assessing, and demonstrating psychology students' professional development. *Teaching of Psychology, 47*(4), 305–315. https://doi.org/10.1177/0098628320945122

Ware, M. E. (2001). Pursuing a career with a bachelor's degree in psychology. In S. Walfish & A. K. Hess (Eds.), *Succeeding in graduate school: The career guide for psychology students* (pp. 11–29).

Wegenek, A. R., & Buskist, W. (2010). *The insider's guide to the psychology major: Everything you need to know about the degree and profession.*

Whitmore, J. (2005). *Business class: Etiquette essentials for success at work.*

Wilcox, M. M., Barbaro-Kukade, L., Pietrantonio, K. R., Franks, D. N., & Davis, B. L. (2021). It takes money to make money: Inequity in psychology graduate student borrowing and financial stressors. *Training and Education in Professional Psychology, 15*(1), 2–17. https://doi.org/10.1037/tep0000294

Williams-Nickelson, C., Prinstein, M. J., & Keilin, W. G. (2019). Goals, essays, and the cover letter. In *Internships in psychology: The APAGS workbook for writing successful applications and finding the right fit* (4th ed.).

Yu, M. C., Kuncel, N. R., & Sackett, P. R. (2020). Some roads lead to psychology, some lead away: College student characteristics and psychology major choice. *Perspectives on Psychological Science, 15*(3), 761–777. https://doi.org/10.1177/1745691619898843